# THE EVOLUTION OF
# DIPLOMATIC METHOD

# THE EVOLUTION OF
# DIPLOMATIC METHOD

*by*

## HAROLD NICOLSON

*Being the Chichele Lectures*
*delivered at*
*the University of Oxford*
*in November 1953*

GREENWOOD PRESS, PUBLISHERS
WESTPORT, CONNECTICUT

**Library of Congress Cataloging in Publication Data**

Nicolson, Harold George, Sir, 1886-1968.
 The evolution of diplomatic method, being the
Chichele lectures delivered at the University of
Oxford in November 1953.

 Reprint of the 1954 ed. published by Constable,
London.
 1. Diplomacy--History.  I.  Title.
[JX1635.N5  1977]      327'.2'09       76-56181
ISBN 0-8371-9428-8

Originally published in 1954 by Constable & Co., Ltd., London

Reprinted with the permission of Constable & Company Ltd.

Reprinted in 1977 by Greenwood Press, Inc.

Library of Congress Catalog Card Number  76-56181

ISBN 0-8371-9428-8

Printed in the United States of America

# CONTENTS

# I

## DIPLOMACY IN GREECE AND ROME

WHEN I was honoured by the invitation to give these lectures, I decided to choose a diplomatic subject. Having spent much of my life in the practice and study of diplomacy, I felt I might be able to illustrate the theme by comparisons drawn from personal experience. I also felt that the eponym of these lectures, while he has received full credit as an ecclesiastic and a lawyer, has not been sufficiently recognised as a diplomatist. It is appropriate to recall that Archbishop Chichele served as Ambassador to the Holy See and France, that in 1409 he was head of the English delegation to the Council of Pisa, and that seven years later he negotiated an alliance between Sigismund, King of the Romans, and Henry V. It is thus fitting that diplomacy also should be celebrated as among the many accomplishments in which the archbishop excelled.

I have chosen as the general title for these four lectures 'The evolution of diplomatic method'. The word 'evolution' is not intended to suggest a continuous progression from the rudimentary to the efficient: on the contrary, I hope to show that international intercourse has always been subject to strange retrogressions. The words 'diplomacy' and 'diplomatic' will be used to designate, neither foreign policy nor international law, but the art of negotiation. And the word 'method' will include, not only the actual machinery for negotiation, but also the general theory, in accordance with which the machinery was used.

I shall divide my lectures into four periods, each representing a definite stage of development. In this, my first lecture, I shall consider the diplomatic method practised in Greece and Rome. My second lecture will be devoted to the unfortunate ideas and habits introduced by the Italians of the fifteenth and sixteenth centuries. In my third lecture I shall examine the improved methods and theories established by the French in the seventeenth, eighteenth and nineteenth centuries. And my last lecture will deal with the innovations in diplomatic method that we have witnessed since 1919.

2

The origins of diplomacy lie buried in the darkness preceding what we call 'the dawn of history'. There came a stage when the anthropoid apes inhabiting one group of caves realised that it might be profitable to reach some understanding with neighbouring groups regarding the limits of their respective hunting territories. Such boundary conventions exist in the animal world, and notably among the smaller birds. It must soon have been realised that no negotiation could reach a satisfactory conclusion if the emissaries of either party were murdered on arrival. Thus the first principle to become firmly established was that of diplomatic immunity. We find it among the Australian aborigines, in the Institutes of Manu, and as an accepted principle in the Homeric poems, when heralds were regarded as possessing special sanctity conferred upon them, not by Hermes only, but by Zeus himself.

That the Greeks at an early stage evolved an elaborate system of diplomatic intercourse is shown by the number of words they invented to differentiate between the various stages and types of agreement.

There was first the διαλλαγή or 'reconciliation', indicating little more than a common desire for the cessation of hostilities. Then came the σύνταξις or arrangement, leading to a temporary local truce. That might be followed, either by a compact, ὁμολογία, or by a convention, συνθήκη. An alliance was called a συμμαχία and a commercial treaty a σύμβολον. The solemn sacred Truce, such as obtained at the period of the Olympic Games was the Σπονδή. Finally there came the lovely word, εἰρήνη, signifying the conclusion of peace.

In the Homeric poems, moreover, we have two detailed descriptions of a diplomatic mission and one reference to what we should now call 'a Geneva rule'. There is a description of the Embassy undertaken, before the war, by Menelaus and Odysseus, when they came to Troy in the hope of securing the restitution of Helen by peaceful means. Their mission failed, owing to the fact that Antimachus, who was in the pay of Paris, organised in the Assembly a majority against the proposal that Helen should be handed back to her husband. Antimachus went so far as to suggest that the ambassadors should be put to death. The story was told (somewhat tactlessly perhaps) by old King Priam to Helen when, several years later, they were sitting together by the Scaean Gates. Odysseus seems to have adopted the irritating diplomatic device of appearing more stupid than he really was. The passage (which recalls for me the slow diffidence with which M. Aristide Briand would climb the steps of the rostrum at Geneva) deserves to be quoted:

'But when before the Assembly of the Trojans the Ambassadors began to weave the web of oratory and persuasion, Menelaus, although the younger of the two, spoke fluently, lucidly, and with few words. Since he was not a garrulous man or one given to digressions. On the other hand, the resourceful Odysseus kept his eyes on the ground when he rose to speak, and held his staff rigidly in his hand, moving it neither to right nor to left, as if he were slow-witted. You would have taken him to be either sulky or stupid. But once you heard that great voice booming from his chest, and when the words fell one after the other like snow-flakes on a winter's day, you realised that Odysseus, as an Ambassador, was beyond compare.'

There are three items in this story that render it relevant to my theme. It indicates that, let us say in 800 B.C., foreign Embassies were generally received by the Assembly as a whole. It shows that they were composed of at least two ambassadors, each of whom delivered his own set speech. And it tells us that Antimachus' proposal that they should violate the diplomatic immunity of the two envoys and put them to death was profoundly shocking to contemporary opinion. When, on a subsequent occasion, the two sons of Antimachus found themselves at the mercy of Agamemnon, having fallen from their chariot in battle, he refused to listen to their whimperings, but cut off their heads in retribution for their father's outrageous suggestion:

*Νῦν μὲν δὴ τοῦ πατρός ἀεικέα τίσετε λώβην.*

The second Homeric description of a diplomatic mission occurs in the 9th Iliad and tells how Ajax, Odysseus and Phoenix went on a mission of appeasement to Achilles in his retirement among the tents of the Myrmidons. This account also provides three useful items of information. Although they were visiting an ally and a friend, they were preceded by two heralds in order to secure immunity and to give religious sanction to the occasion. They received their instructions, not from the general Assembly, but from the smaller Council, not from Parliament, but from the Cabinet. And although Phoenix came with them, there is evidence to suggest that Ajax and Odysseus only had the status of accredited ambassadors. Obviously the diplomatic machinery of pre-historic times was more elaborate than is sometimes assumed.

There seems also to have existed a religious sanction, mitigating the unrestrained barbarities of war and analogous to our Geneva Convention. Thus Homer tells us that when Ilus snubbed Odysseus because the latter asked him for a poison in which to dip his arrows, he did so 'because he stood in awe of the Gods'. Thus, even in the heroic age, there did exist certain international principles, the violation of which was regarded with distaste.

### 3

In the few, but vividly illumined years, that stretch between Marathon and Chaeronea, the Greeks developed many methods of negotiation in regard to which we possess detailed information.

Although the system of establishing permanent missions resident in the capital of a foreign country was only adopted fourteen hundred years later, the Greek cities were constantly sending and receiving embassies of a temporary, or *ad hoc*, character. Ambassadors, who were called 'elders', were chosen for their known respectability and reputed wisdom, and in some cities it was laid down that they should not be under fifty years of age. They were given credentials by the Assembly, a specimen of which can be seen in the Ashmolean in this town; any person claiming to be an Ambassador without having received such credentials was liable to be put to death. They were accorded very meagre travelling allowances and were not supposed to accept presents. Timagoras of Athens was executed for receiving presents from King Artaxerxes and Demosthenes used all his gifts of innuendo to suggest that Aeschines had been bribed by Philip of Macedon. If their negotiations were successful, and approved by their fellow citizens, they were rewarded by a garland of wild olive, a free meal in the town hall, and sometimes a commemorative tablet. If unsuccessful, all manner of penalties might be imposed. In any case they were obliged to submit their expense account to disobliging scrutiny on the part of the Public Accounts Committee, and their political enemies might take this occasion to indict them for corruption or for παραπρεσβεία, namely 'incompetent diplomacy'. It was thus no sinecure to serve as the ambassador of a Greek City State.

So suspicious was Greek democracy of its own diplomatists, that missions were composed of several ambassadors, representing different parties and points of view. In place of the unity of impression that any effective embassy should convey, a Greek Mission suggested a sharp concentration of party animosities. For instance, we learn from Aeschines that Demosthenes, when serving on an extremely important embassy to the Court of Macedon, was on such bad terms with his colleagues that he refused to sit at the same table with them, or to sleep in the same house. It was thus easy for those with whom such mixed embassies were negotiating to play upon these personal animosities and to divide the mission against itself. It seems curious to us that intelligent people should have permitted so bad a diplomatic method to survive.

During the period of Greek liberty, diplomatic negotiations were conducted orally and, at least in theory, with full publicity. The several members of an Embassy (there were often as many as ten Ambassadors in a single mission) would each deliver a set speech to a foreign monarch or Assembly, much as happens in the ill-ordered international Conferences of today. If the negotiations resulted in a treaty, the terms of that treaty were engraved in pure attic on a tablet for all to see. Its ratification was accomplished by the public exchange of solemn oaths. Thus it could certainly be said that the Greeks adopted the system of open covenants openly arrived at. When Macedonian ascendancy was established, and the old attic was replaced by the *koiné*, or *lingua franca*, the full terms of treaties were not invariably published. The pernicious system of secret treaties, as that between Athens and King Philip regarding Amphipolis, thus crept in.

It might be supposed that the Greek Cities, with their extreme exclusiveness, would have been opposed to such middle courses as neutrality and arbitration. In fact, the status of neutrality, which they designated by the vivid verb 'to stay quiet', was a clearly defined status, whereas arbitration was for them a quite customary device for securing the pacific settlement of disputes. There still exists the text of a Treaty between Athens and Thebes, in one article of which the city of Lamia is designated as 'the chosen city' to act as arbiter between them. Sometimes an individual was nominated arbiter;—a philosopher of international repute, or even a victor at the Olympic games. As many as 46 cases of arbitration are recorded as having been adjudicated between 300 and 100 B.C.

One of the most useful institutions developed by the Greeks was that of the consul, or Proxenos. Unlike most consuls today, the Proxenos was a native of the city in which he resided and was expected there to further and protect the interests of the citizens of the State by which he was appointed. The post of Proxenos was regarded as one of honour and many distinguished men were glad to serve in that capacity; thus Pindar became the Proxenos of Athens at Thebes, and Demosthenes the Proxenos of Thebes at Athens. The post tended to become hereditary and the institution served, not merely to assist merchants visiting a foreign city, but also to initiate diplomatic negotiations and to assuage the internecine bitterness by which the Hellenic world was sundered and envenomed.

By the fifth century the Greeks had undoubtedly acquired an elaborate apparatus of international intercourse. They had their Amphictyonic Councils, their leagues and their alliances, showing that, in theory at least, they recognised the value of combination: they had evolved accepted principles covering such matters as the declaration of war, the conclusion of peace, the ratification of treaties, arbitration, neutrality, the exchange of ambassadors, the functions of a consul, and certain rules of war: they had also worked out regulations, which were widely observed, defining the position of aliens, the grant of naturalization, the right of asylum, extradition, and maritime practices.

It is not however sufficient to possess a machine; what is important is the purposes for which that machine is employed and the spirit in which it is operated. What, in other words, was the Greek diplomatic idea?

## 4

It is sometimes said that the Hellenic world possessed no conception of international concord or ethics, without which even the most perfect diplomatic machine is bound to prove unworkable. It is true that the average Greek's loyalty to his own city was so intensive, that he regarded all other Hellenes as potential enemies, and all barbarians as natural slaves. It is true also that he drew a sharp distinction between private and public morality, and that it would never have occurred to him that Demosthenes was being cynical in asserting that: 'Our purposes and our actions must invariably be just: yet we must be careful to see that they are also attended with advantage.'

Yet, in spite of their belief that the safety of their own City constituted the supreme law, the Greeks did recognise the existence of certain divinely ordained principles governing the conduct of international affairs. Treaties were under the special guardianship of Zeus Pistios, and it was thought wrong to break a treaty without good reason, or to abandon an ally in the middle of a campaign. The Cretans, the Thessalians, the Parians, even the Spartans, were universally condemned for their diplomatic unreliability. It was regarded as impious to make a surprise attack upon a neighbour or to start what they called 'an unheralded and truceless war'. Atrocities committed against the wounded or the dead in battle were condemned as worthy only of barbarians. And they did dimly realize that, apart from τὰ τῶν Ἑλλήνων νόμιμα, namely the laws and customs maintaining among members of the Hellenic community, there existed certain πάντων ἀνθρώπων νόμιμα, namely principles applying to all mankind. They may even, occasionally, have agreed with the verdict of Thucydides that war, as a means of settling international disputes, was 'neither good nor safe'.

In spite of these excellent concepts, they made a mess of their diplomacy and for three obvious reasons.

In the first place, they were afflicted with what Herodian has called 'that ancient malady of the Greeks, the love of discord'. Their jealousy was so poisonous that it stung and paralysed their instinct for self-preservation. In the second place the Greeks were not by temperament good diplomatists, but bad diplomatists. Being an amazingly clever people, they ascribed a wrong value to ingenuity and stratagem, thereby destroying the basis of all sound negotiation, which is confidence. They were moreover tactless and garrulous; they lacked all sense of occasion; and they were woefully indiscreet. To find a parallel, for instance, for the indiscretion of Demosthenes one has to skip two thousand years of civilization and seek for examples among our own contemporaries. In the third place they failed, in their external as in their internal affairs, to establish a correct distribution of responsibility between the Legislature and the executive. They never discovered, as we ourselves have not yet discovered, how to render the diplomatic method of a democracy as efficient as that of an autocracy. It was this final fault that brought them to ruin.

A democracy, when dealing with a despotic system, is always at a disadvantage, since its decisions can never be either so secret or so quick. The Greeks, owing to the cumbrous methods they adopted, magnified this disadvantage. In that their ambassadors were practically never accorded full powers, they had either to return to their home cities, or send messengers, in order to obtain the additional instructions which the development of the situation might necessitate. In those days of slow communications the delay thereby entailed might prove disastrous. The Assembly itself was irresponsible and volatile and might easily repudiate its ambassadors, even when they had strictly adhered to their instructions.

An almost perfect illustration of the delays and confusions inherent in democratic diplomacy is provided by the series of panic-stricken negotiations that took place between the city of Athens and Philip of Macedon on the eve of the final catastrophe. On the one hand, there were the Greek City States, terrified by the vast new armament that Philip had accumulated, yet unwilling to combine together in resistance to the northern barbarian, and each prepared at any moment to sell the other out. On the other hand you had the King of Macedonia—resolute, astute, and absolute master of his own plans and army—conscious of the fear and discord that his threats had produced among

the Hellenic communities,—aware that each one of
these frightened cities would welcome as applying to
themselves the promises and assurances that he so
lavishly distributed,—and only too willing to prolong
diplomatic conversations while he himself occupied
strategic positions one by one. Amphipolis, Olynthus,
Cersobletes, Euboea, the great Amphictyony of
Delphi, Thermopylae itself—one by one they fell
under the control of Macedon, while the Assembly at
Athens were condemning unsuccessful ambassadors
to death, holding turbulent sessions to discuss the despatch of new embassies with fresh instructions,
grasping at promises which they knew to be false or at
hopes which they knew to be fallacious, and destroying
such confidence as their allies still placed in their
sagacity and fortitude.

In the indictment which Demosthenes delivered
against his former colleague, Aeschines, which we
possess under the name of *De Falsa Legatione*, there
are passages which, while they recall to us the dilemma
that faced our own Government in 1938, constitute a
serious criticism of Greek diplomatic method. In this
speech Demosthenes was ostensibly prosecuting Aeschines for παραπρεσβεία, for wilful dilatoriness, for
undue, and seemingly corrupt, reliance upon Philip's
verbal assurances, and for misinforming the Assembly
on his return. It would have been difficult for Demosthenes, as it would be difficult for a United States
Senator today, to place the blame for these misfortunes
on the faults of the constitution, or on the ignorance,
gullibility, cowardice and suspicion of the Athenian
Assembly. In assailing Aeschines he was assailing an
inefficient diplomatic system and his criticism is not

wholly irrelevant today. Let me quote some of his passages:

'Ambassadors,' said Demosthenes, 'have no battleships at their disposal, or heavy infantry, or fortresses; their weapons are words and opportunities. In important transactions opportunities are fleeting; once they are missed they cannot be recovered. It is a greater offence to deprive a democracy of an opportunity than it would be thus to deprive an oligarchy or an autocracy. Under their systems, action can be taken instantly and on the word of command; but with us, first the Council has to be notified and adopt a provisional resolution, and even then only when the heralds and the Ambassadors have sent in a note in writing. Then the Council has to convene the Assembly, but then only on a statutory date. Then the debater has to prove his case in face of an ignorant and often corrupt opposition; and even when this endless procedure has been completed, and a decision has been come to, even more time is wasted before the necessary financial resolution can be passed. Thus an ambassador who, in a constitution such as ours, acts in a dilatory manner and causes us to miss our opportunities, is not missing opportunities only, but robbing us of the control of events. . . . It seems to me, men of Athens, that you have become absolutely apathetic, waiting there dumbly for the catastrophe that is about to fall upon you. There you sit, observing the disasters that overwhelm your neighbours and taking no measures for your own defence! Nor do you seem conscious even of the elaborate methods by which your country is slowly being undermined.'

Demosthenes may have been wrong in his estimate of the foreign policy which Athens, in then existing conditions, ought to have pursued. But he was certainly not wrong in his indictment of the diplomatic method which that great democracy had evolved.

This incompetence led straight to Chaeronea; and to that barbaric night after the battle, when Philip and his generals, drunk with wine and victory, reeled out of the royal tent, hiccupping to each other the jingle 'Demosthenes, Demosthenous', and slithering over the corpses of Athenians, piled naked under the moon.

5

We might have supposed that the Romans, with their practical good-sense and their excellent capacity for administration, would have devised and maintained a more exemplary diplomatic method. But even as the Greeks failed owing to natural protervity and inefficient institutions, so also did the Romans fail owing to the fault of masterfulness. I am not suggesting that the Roman Empire and the Pax Romana were anything but magnificent benefits, for which we of the civilised world should remain eternally grateful. I am suggesting only that, in seeking to impose their will, rather than to negotiate on a basis of reciprocity, the Romans did not develop a diplomatic method, valuable enough to figure among the many gifts that they bequeathed to posterity.

It is true that, with their passion for categories and their love of juridical formulas, they invented a number of phrases suggestive of the most elevated conception of international relationships and of an ordered method by which such relationships might be conducted. They were always, for instance, boasting of their own good faith, their *prisca fides*, and contrasting it with the inveterate duplicity of their opponents. Every Roman schoolboy was taught to admire the straightforwardness of the Senate in handing back to the Samnites the generals who had signed the repudiated armistice of the Caudine Forks. Every Roman was moved by the magnificent example of Regulus returning unperturbed to Carthage rather than break his word. Frequently would the Romans refer to the *civitas gentium*, or the *ius gentium*, but the former was little more than a sentimental phrase, and the latter did not, as Grotius and others have supposed, always form the foundation of international law, but was more often a body of excellent rules governing the relations between foreigners and Roman citizens.

It is true also that they regarded treaties as in the nature of a legal contract: indeed they would often rely on their juridical ingenuity to evade terms that had been signed and ratified. But the College of Fetials, and the *ius fetiale*, were little more than an archaic survival. At best they performed functions, analagous to those of the Treaty Department in our own Foreign Office, namely preserving treaty documents, dealing with matters of protocol, and seeing to it that war was declared, or peace concluded, in proper ceremonial form. The procedure established by the Fetials reads like a passage from the Golden Bough. When war was to be declared, the *pater patratus* would journey to the enemy frontier and hurl across it a spear fashioned of cornel wood hardened in fire; or, if time were short and the frontier distant, he would go through the same operation in front of the Temple of Bellona. If peace were to be concluded, the same official, bearing the sceptre of Jupiter Feretrius, and accompanied by the *pater verbenarius*, who carried with him a spring of sacred verbena from the herb-garden on the Capitol, would cause the treaty to be read aloud to the ambassadors of the other contracting party, would pronounce a curse upon anyone who dared in future to violate its terms, and would then cut the throat of a sow with the *lapis silex*, evidently some neolithic dagger of immense antiquity. It is not surprising that Suetonius, when telling us that the Emperor Claudius personally revived this practice, should do so with a slightly supercilious sneer.

It is true again that in the very early days of the Republic the Romans entered into treaties on a reciprocal basis and that the original Latin Confederation began as a coalition of equals. But very soon we find that it was in the Capitol at Rome that auspices were taken on behalf of the whole League, and that decisions were there adopted without the knowledge or consent of the smaller allies. Gradually the old form of coalition, associated with such words as *amicitia*, *foedus*, or *societas*, was succeeded by new forms, under which the federated parties were constrained to recognize the *maiestas populi romani*, or, in more modern terms, to surrender to the Roman Senate the control of foreign policy and defence. In coalitions comprising one dominant Power and a number of subsidiary satellites, the methods of diplomacy, which imply the acceptance of the principle of reciprocity between sovereign and independent States, tend to languish and then to disappear. Gradually, as Livy observed, the Senate came to regard the expedient as more important than the just, to prefer the *utile* to the *honestum*: and for them the *utile* was any measure that furthered the expansion of the influence and power of Rome.

6

The Roman doctrine of imperialism, the belief that it was their destiny to impose on other nations the habits of the *pax romana*, that it was their duty to crush all opposition and to spare only those who surrendered to their dominance, did not enable them to develop or bequeath to their successors, any exemplary body of diplomatic maxims. The most that can be said is that they did inculcate a theoretical respect for good-faith, and an understanding of the purely practical importance of reliable contracts. Such contributions as they made to diplomatic theory were either not commendable in themselves, or not relevant to a world consisting of national States, each claiming the status of equality. Yet, with their great gifts for organization, they did certainly introduce some improvement into the diplomatic machine as used, or misused, by the Greek City States.

Their ambassadors, who were called either *nuntii* or *oratores*, were appointed by the Senate, by whom they were provided with credentials and instructions. Only rarely were they accorded full powers, and an ambassador who exceeded his *auctoritas* could be impeached. Ambassadors were usually of senatorial rank, or chosen from the more distinguished of the Knights; the Rhodians were deeply hurt when the Senate sent them an ambassador who was a gymnastic instructor in private life, a precursor, it would seem, of Conrad Henlein, the leader of the Sudeten Germans. In general, their ambassadors were men of becoming gravity, who were in fact worthy representatives of the formidable dignity of Rome. Their missions were of short duration and on their return they delivered a report to the Senate on the business that they had transacted. The Senate, as we learn from Livy, would then vote on the motion that their business be approved.

The regulations governing the reception of foreign ambassadors in Rome are of greater originality and interest. The immunity accorded by ancient tradition, and by the *ius gentium*, to visiting ambassadors, was extended to include their *comites* or staffs. But it did not, it seems, cover their diplomatic correspondence, which was exposed to scrutiny by the Roman postal officials. Members of a visiting embassy who committed some offence against the law were generally sent back under guard to the country of their origin, there to be dealt with by their own authorities. It was thus regarded as a departure from the accustomed procedure when a junior member of an Embassy from Jugurtha was tried for murder in a Roman court. Disputes affecting the rights and privileges of a foreign diplomatic mission were referred to the College of Fetials, much as the are referred to our own Treaty Department today. It does not seem that the immunity accorded to ambassadors and their staffs extended to their residences or their servants. It must be remembered, however, that in those days there was no such thing as a resident ambassador, possessing an embassy and household of his own. Visiting ambassadors were accommodated on arrival in a reception centre, called the 'Graecostasis', and their domestic requirements, including a staff of servants, were provided by the State.

As the self-confidence and power of Rome in-

creased, embassies from abroad were treated with
varying degrees of contumely. An enemy potentate or
tribe, anxious to sue for peace, had first to obtain from
the local Roman General permission to send an embassy to the Senate. Their envoys, on arrival, had to
wait outside the city in some rat-infested inn until the
Senate signified that they might enter. Their reception,
if and when it occurred, took place in the Temple of
Bellona. Even an embassy from a friendly and theoreti-
cally equal Power was obliged, on reaching the out-
skirts of Rome, to notify its presence to the *quaestor
urbanus*, and to solicit permission to enter. If this were
accorded, the ambassadors and their staffs were taken
to the Graecostasis, where they waited patiently until
their audience with the Senate could be arranged. They
were then conducted to the Curia and were allowed to
address the Senate, if necessary through an interpreter.
An interesting innovation was that individual Senators
were permitted to put questions to the Ambassadors
after the conclusion of their address. The Embassy was
then conducted back to the Graecostasis, and eventually summoned to return to the Curia to receive the
Senatorial reply. There is little in all this to suggest any marked improvement on the old Greek
system.

It might happen, (as it did happen to the Carthaginian Ambassadors who came to Rome in 205 B.C.,)
that the Senate refused to recognize a visiting Embassy or to hear what they had to say. In that event,
they were deprived of their diplomatic immunity, de-
nounced as spies or '*speculatores*', and conducted under
armed guard to the coast. This is fortunately not a
diplomatic practice that survived into a later age.

There were other innovations that the Romans introduced. They set up a court of *Recuperatores*, consisting of two judges representing each party to a treaty, with a neutral chairman. Some authorities have seen in this institution, of which in fact little is known, the origins of an arbitral tribunal. It is doubtful, however, whether the Court of *Recuperatores* possessed any political, diplomatic, or arbitral functions: it seems to have constituted little more than what we should now call a Mixed Commission for the adjudication of Claims.

Another, and far less admirable practice developed by the Romans, was that of inserting in a Treaty provisions regarding the delivery of hostages as guarantors of its execution. When, after the Second Punic War the Romans, being undisputed masters of the world, felt no need for reciprocity in their dealings with other countries, they demanded hostages from conquered tribes and peoples, but never under any circumstances delivered any themselves. Even Julius Caesar, who was regarded by his contemporaries as the gentlest of all warriors, exacted as many as 600 hostages from the Gallic tribes. Articles were inserted in treaties, prescribing the number of hostages to be delivered, their names and quality, the sex and age-groups to which they should belong, and whether they could be replaced by others after a certain number of years. The Romans found by experience that the barbarians minded far more delivering up female hostages than they resented the demand for male hostages. So long as a conquered tribe or nation respected the terms of their surrender, the hostages were well treated and assuredly benefited much from their enforced sojourn in Rome. But if the terms of the treaty were broken, then the hostages were immediately arrested and treated as prisoners of war.

This system of delivering hostages as guarantors of a treaty, which is inequitable in itself and not to be recommended either in peace or war, persisted long after Roman times. Under the terms of the Treaty of Aix-la-Chapelle of 1748, two British peers, Lord Suffolk and the young Lord Cathcart, were delivered as hostages for the return of Cap Breton to France. They spent months in Paris, idling sheepishly in the taverns and theatres of the town, and regarded by French society with not unkindly amusement. Since those days, the device of taking hostages has been employed for military, rather than for diplomatic, purposes.

An equally interesting innovation, but one which can be applied only by a Power dominant in peace and war, was that of setting an exact time limit to negotiations. Thus the Macedonian ambassadors who came to Rome in 197 B.C. were informed on arrival that, unless the negotiations resulted in agreement within sixty days, they would be regarded, not as a diplomatic mission enjoying immunity, but as spies or '*speculatores*', and as such, conducted under armed guard to the coast. This form of ultimatum, (however enticing may be its appeal to future negotiators,) is not one which today could be employed with equal directness: more silky methods have now to be devised to forestall or prevent deliberate procrastination.

What lessons, therefore, can we learn from the diplomatic practices of antiquity? I have directed attention to the three main merits and the three main defects of the system evolved by the Greek City States. In theory at least, the Greeks discovered that international relations must be governed by certain stable principles. They did much to develop the actual machinery of diplomacy and international law. And their insistence that Covenants should be openly arrived at did preserve them at least during their period of liberty, from the curse of secret treaties. On the other hand they failed entirely to mitigate the disadvantages inseparable from democratic diplomacy in its dealings with despotic governments. In that the Assembly was the sovereign authority. their negotiations were exposed to the decisions, at once cumbrous and volatile, of a body of citizens, who were extremely ill-informed, subject to gusts of anger, sentimentality, fear or suspicion, inclined at any moment to reverse previous attitudes, and disastrously slow at coming to any decision. The sole remedy for such defects would have been the creation of a body of trained negotiators, independent of party allegiances and passions, inspiring general confidence, but ultimately subject to the authority of the State. In place of this, their embassies were composed of active politicians, bitterly hostile to each other, underpaid and therefore subject to pecuniary inducements, and exposed to heavy penalties if on their return they failed to convince the Assembly of their success.

The Romans, on the other hand, did much to introduce order into international relations and to establish the doctrine of the sanctity of contract. Yet even in Republican times they were too dictatorial to appreciate diplomatic niceties and too masterful to bequeath valuable examples or lessons, such as might have helped posterity to evolve a sound method of negotiation. The systems of antiquity were none the less preferable to the wolf-like habits developed by the Italians of the Renaissance. It is these habits that I propose to examine in my next lecture.

# II

## THE ITALIAN SYSTEM

### I

With the disintegration of the Roman Empire and the emergence, both in the East and the West, of a number of autonomous and aggressive barbarian nations, the old habit of acquiescence imposed by the *pax romana* was succeeded by a new spirit of competition. Policy ceased to be stated in the sharp alternatives of obedience or revolt, but became a question of adjusting rival ambitions, or of fortifying national security, by the conciliation of enemies and the acquisition of allies. It was then that professional diplomacy,—an art which the Greeks had been too insolent, and the Romans too haughty, to study or perfect—became one of the branches of statesmanship. It was a misfortune that this art, so necessary for the relations between self-governing communities, came to Europe, neither illumined by Athenian intelligence, nor dignified by Roman seriousness, but falsified and discredited by the practices of oriental Courts.

It was the Byzantines who taught diplomacy to Venice; it was the Venetians who set the pattern for the Italian cities, for France and Spain, and eventually for all Europe. It was an intricate and unreasonable pattern; it was a pattern that ignored the practical purposes of true negotiation, and introduced an abominable filigree of artifice into what ought always to be a simple machine.

The Byzantine Emperors were the first to organize a special department of government for dealing with external affairs, and to train professional negotiators to serve as their ambassadors to foreign courts. These envoys were furnished with written 'instructions' and were told to be invariably courteous in their dealings with foreigners and never to criticise, but rather to praise, conditions that they observed abroad. On the accession of a new Emperor, special Embassies were despatched to announce this event: and the expenses of these missions were defrayed by allowing the envoys to take with them bales of merchandize which they sold for local currency on arrival. This economic device, although copied by the Venetians in some cases, did not survive in future diplomatic practice. It was found that ambassadors whose missions were financed by such a method tended to devote more attention to trading profits than they did to the task of negotiation. But other Byzantine habits infected diplomatic method for many centuries to come.

There was in the first place the extreme importance attached at Byzantium to questions of protocol and ceremonial. The Emperor Constantine Porphyrogenitus wrote a long treatise on the subject which appears to have served as a manual for his successors. A special department, called the 'Skrinion Barbarôn' was created to arrange for the reception of foreign ambassadors and to see to it that they were suitably impressed and suitably invigilated. On their arrival at Constantinople, foreign ambassadors and their staffs were interned in conditions of extreme luxury in a special building, the *Xenodochium Romanorum*, where their movements, visitors and communications were carefully scrutinised by a guard of honour composed entirely of the secret police. The ceremony of their reception was organised with splendour and fraud. In order that they might return impressed by the military might of Byzantium, they were obliged to attend an interminable review at which the same troops, emerging from one of the gates and entering by another, came round and round again carrying different types of armour. In order to dazzle them with the glamour and mystery of the Emperor, mechanical devices caused the lions flanking the steps of his throne to roar terribly, while the throne itself worked up and down as if on a lift, so that the visiting ambassador, on rising from the kow-tow or προσκυνήσις (in itself a loathesome oriental innovation) would notice that the Emperor had been miraculously elevated since first observed. Nor was the ambassador permitted at his first audience to address the Emperor directly: such compliments as were exchanged were transmitted through the Logothetes.

There exists an entertaining, scurrilous, and perhaps unreliable, account of a diplomatic mission undertaken to Byzantium in A.D. 968. It was written by Luitprand, Bishop of Cremona, who was sent to persuade the Emperor Nicephorus Phocas to agree to the marriage of the son of Otto I with Princess Theophano, daughter of the late Emperor Romanos. In his *Relatio de Legatione Constantinopolitana*, Bishop Luitprand recounts the failure of his mission with remarkable gusto. He de-

scribes Nicephorus Phocas as a toad-like figure of re-
pulsive appearance, who had the audacity to question
whether Otto had any right at all to style himself
Roman Emperor. He retails in lavish detail the re-
proaches which he, as a loyal servant of his German
master, hurled back at the disgusting Byzantine. This
is the first, although not the last, example of negotiation
by insult.

2

The Venetians, owing to their long and intimate
relations with the East, became indoctrinated with the
Byzantine theory of diplomacy and transmitted to their
fellow Italians the oriental defects of duplicity and suspicion. They were the first to create an organised
system of diplomacy, and as late as 1740 we find Lord
Chesterfield advising his son to frequent Venetian
Ambassadors when abroad, since of all the diplomatic
body they could be counted upon to be the most
polished and the best informed. Let me shortly
examine the principles and practices which the
Venetians devised.

They were the first, and it is much to their credit, to
preserve their state archives in systematic form. Their
diplomatic documents cover the nine centuries from
883 to 1797 and contain the instructions given to, and
the official despatches received from, the ambassadors
sent to foreign countries. As many as 21,177 of such
despatches are still preserved. They were carefully
summarised and indexed in registers called 'rubricarii'.
The archives also contain the final reports, addressed
by ambassadors to the Signory on the completion of
their missions. There were in addition what were called

*avvisi*, or news-letters, by which ambassadors abroad were kept informed of events at home. The Venetians were thus the first to realize that ambassadors are apt to fall out of touch with affairs and opinions in their own country, and that their representative value is to that extent diminished. In our own service, this excellent practice was extended to include the circulation in print to all missions abroad, of copies of important despatches and telegrams received from all other missions. Our Ambassador at Stockholm, for instance, on reading 'the print' sent him in his fortnightly diplomatic bag, would learn exactly the nature and scope of negotiations then proceeding in Tokyo or Washington. He was thus kept regularly informed of the diplomatic weather-chart as a whole, and not merely of that sector of it with which he was personally concerned. This invaluable practice, which has since been imitated by other Governments, derives essentially from the Venetian custom of keeping their missions abroad supplied with regular *avvisi*, or news-letters.

Other Venetian practices were less worthy of imitation. Their regulations governing the appointment and conduct of ambassadors date from as far back as 1268 and 1288 and provide us with an indication of what they regarded as the correct diplomatic method. A Venetian ambassador was appointed for three or four months only, a period which in the fifteenth century was extended to a possible limit of two years. He was not allowed to possess any property in the country to which he was sent, and any presents he might receive had to be handed to the Signory on his return. He was not accorded any leave of absence whatsoever and had to deliver his final report to the Signory not less than fifteen days after the completion of his mission. He was forbidden to take his wife with him, since she might gossip, and ordained to take his own cook, since foreign cooks might seek to poison him.

The post of Venetian Ambassador, at least until the sixteenth century, was not therefore one that was accepted with any alacrity. It entailed heavy expense, separation from domestic comforts and affections, absence from the political struggle at home, exposure to hard travelling, brigands, atrocious inns, and the various illnesses that raged in foreign parts. It is not surprising that the acceptance of an embassy had to be rendered compulsory. A decree of 1271 imposed a heavy fine, increased by subsequent decrees, on any Venetian who refused to undertake an embassy when ordered to do so. We find a similar ordinance in the Florentine 'Regulations for Ambassadors' of 1421. Any citizen who, when appointed Ambassador, was not 'prompt and obedient' in leaving for his post, was exposed to severe penalties, including even the loss of civic rights. As late as the sixteenth century, we find Guicciardini deploring the fact that the more important Florentines managed to evade being sent on diplomatic missions and that the Government was thus obliged to recruit their ambassadors from the ranks of clerks and functionaries. Guicciardini was evidently thinking of that capable and industrious civil servant, Niccolò Machiavelli.

Even more revealing are the regulations imposed by the Venetians as a result of their conviction that all foreigners, and especially all foreign diplomatists, had come to spy. A regulation of 1481 forbade Venetian Ambassadors to discuss politics with any unofficial foreigner or to mention them in their private letters home. In the next year, sentence of banishment, and a fine of 2000 ducats, were decreed as penalties on any Venetian citizen who ventured to discuss public affairs with a foreign diplomatist. This senseless custom of regarding foreign missions as dangerous emissaries, to be strictly avoided as if they were lepers, lapsed during the age of reason. In the less civilised sections of the world it has been revived in recent times.

### 3

The year 1492 is an important date in the evolution of diplomatic method. In that year Lorenzo de Medici died and a Borgia became Pope. Until then, the great Florentine had been the accepted guardian of peace in Italy: until then the Holy Father had been revered as the spiritual mediator between nations, as the natural chairman of some divinely appointed arbitral tribunal. Even as the Pope was regarded as ruling the conscience of all mankind, so also was the Holy Roman Emperor regarded as representing, at least in theory, the old conception of universal sovereignty. Once the Pope began himself to indulge in power politics, once the Emperor ceased to possess undisputed authority, the field was open for feverish competition between the small Italian States. Even the ancient principle of a united Christendom arrayed against the infidel succumbed to the growing appetite for riches. Venice and Genoa vied with each other in establishing commercial relations with the Ottoman Sultan; and on February 25 1500 a Turkish Ambassador was received in the Vatican itself. Meanwhile Louis XI, claiming to be an anointed but independent Christian sovereign, had established

France as a third force in Europe. It was he who, long before Machiavelli, asserted the principle that the raison d'Etat was above morality, and who introduced duplicity as an element in diplomatic technique. In sending ambassadors to Brittany he provided them with shameless instructions. 'If they lie to you,' he said, 'see to it that you lie much more to them.' Yet the diplomatic method that emerged from the fifteenth century was essentially an Italian method, and it is as such that it must be examined.

The diverse systems established by the Italian Communities had one common characteristic, namely, that, with the possible exception of Venice, they were physically weak. They possessed nothing comparable to a national army or militia, they relied for their defence on the fluctuating support of mercenaries, they were internally debilitated by the presence of dangerous fifth columns, and when the inevitable foreign invasion came to challenge their disunity, they collapsed almost without a gesture of resistance. They sought to supplement their precarious systems, their lamentable defences, by diplomatic combinations; even to this day, the Italian word '*combinazioni*' has a sinister ring. Knowing their existence to be precarious, these despots and oligarchs aimed at immediate results only; they had no idea at all of the value of long-term policies or of the gradual creation of confidence. To them the art of negotiation became a game of hazard for high immediate stakes; it was conducted in an atmosphere of excitement, and with that combination of cunning, recklessness and ruthlessness which they lauded as 'Virtù'.

The general conception that animated their ceaseless

fiddlings with the balance of power, can be deduced from the works of Machiavelli. We are taught today that it is a mistake to regard this great writer as a cynical man; that we must regard him as an enlightened patriot, dreaming of Italian unity, and shattered by the dread that physical weakness and dissension would destroy all Italian liberties and render permanent in Italy the strife and dominance of foreign Kings. He had recognised in Cesare Borgia the ruthless will, the expert calculation, the speed of decision, that to his mind could alone save Italy from being enslaved by the French, the Spaniards, or the Germans. He was not, we are assured, composing a manual for the guidance of future diplomatists; he was merely writing a 'tract for the times' in which he analysed, with remarkable clarity, the illnesses from which Italy was then suffering. He was not establishing a permanent doctrine; he was expounding *la verità effettuale*, the effective truth, as he experienced it in his own life-time.

This may well be the correct historical manner in which to approach Machiavelli, but it is unfortunate none the less that his influence should have been both so wide and so prolonged. Successive European sovereigns, such as Charles V, Philip II, and Henri Quatre, are known to have taken *Il Principe* as their political guide book; and the general theory that the safety and interests of the State take precedence over all ethical considerations was, in after years, adopted and expanded by great men, such as Hegel and Treitschke, with, as we know, very unfortunate results.

4

Although the contemporaries and successors of Machiavelli did lasting harm to the theory, or ethics, of the art of negotiation, they did much to elaborate, and sometimes to improve, actual diplomatic method. Let me now consider some of the ideas and practices that were evolved, mainly in Italy, during the course of the fifteenth and sixteenth centuries.

The most important, of course, was the establishment of permanent diplomatic missions, with ambassadors resident in the capital of the country to which they were accredited. Although since A.D. 453 the Pope had appointed a permanent representative, or 'Apocrisarius', at the court of Byzantium, and although the Archbishop of Ravenna had for long maintained an envoy, or 'Responsalis' at the Curia in Rome, the first resident embassy in the modern sense was that accredited in 1450 to Cosimo dei Medici by the Duke of Milan. The Ambassador chosen on that occasion was Nicodemus dei Pontramoli, known to his contemporaries as 'sweet Nicodemus'. Within the next fifteen years this example was followed by practically all the Italian and European States. These envoys were not at first called 'ambassadors' but 'resident orators'. In fact the title of ambassador, derived from a Celtic word meaning 'servant',—first used, so far as I know, in the *De Bello Gallico*—became current not earlier than the middle of the sixteenth century, when the Emperor Charles V decreed that it should be accorded only to the representatives of crowned heads and the Republic of Venice, and should not be used to designate the representatives of other republics or free cities.

B                                                    E.D.M.

It was not at first the custom to choose as ambassadors members of the nobility or governing class. Louis XI sent his barber on a mission to Maria of Burgundy, Florence sent a chemist of the name of Matthew Palmerius to Naples, and Dr. de Puebla, who for twenty years represented Spain in London, was so filthy and unkempt that Henry VII expressed the hope that his successor might be a man more fitted for human society. Our own early ambassadors, men such as John Stile and Richard Pace, were often people of quite humble origin. It was the Curia in Rome that first insisted that diplomatists should be drawn from the upper classes: in 1459 Pius II refused to accept the credentials of a foreign envoy on the ground that he was not up to ambassadorial standards, '*quod esset dignitate legationis obscurior.*' Nor in those early days was it considered necessary that an ambassador should be a native of the country which he represented. Henry VIII employed an Italian, Spinelli, as his minister in the Netherlands, and there then existed professional international diplomatists, such as the Pole, Laski, or the Spaniard, Rincon, or the Hungarian Frangipani, who served different masters in turn. In exceptional cases merchants resident in a foreign capital were given the status of 'sub-ambassadors'. Thus Venice appointed two successive sub-ambassadors in London rather than send one of their own patricians, on the ground that 'the journey to the English island is very long and very dangerous'.

Permanent ambassadors were for long regarded with deep suspicion, on the assumption that they might profit by their diplomatic immunity to act as spies. Bacon tells us that Henry VII had such a dislike of foreign ambassadors remaining in England that before his death he had determined to abolish the practice. Philippe de Comines was expressing an opinion which long persisted when he wrote 'It is not at all safe, all this coming and going of ambassadors'. Even as late as 1653 the Swiss Minister accredited to Cromwell reported that any Member of Parliament who spoke to a foreign ambassador was liable to be deprived of his seat. In Moscow in 1660 foreign diplomatists were treated almost as prisoners of war, and in Turkey the Castle of the Seven Towers was kept permanently ready for their accommodation. This suspicion of foreign ambassadors for long contaminated the esteem in which diplomatists were regarded even in their home countries. It was felt that they might have become infected with foreign ways of thought, and have lost their national character. It would be too much to say that this atmosphere of suspicion (essentially an oriental failing) has been entirely dissipated in our own enlightened days. Even in this country a professional diplomatist is regarded as rather un-English; as a queer cosmopolitan; and so he is.

It is interesting to consider what were the special qualities expected of an ambassador in the fifteenth and sixteenth centuries. There exist many contemporary manuals and memoirs indicating that the mental and moral equipment of a good diplomatist must comprise at least the following nine ingredients. He must be a good linguist and above all a master of Latin, which was still the *lingua franca* of the time. He must realize that all foreigners are regarded with suspicion and must therefore conceal his astuteness and appear as a pleasant man of the world. He must be hospitable and employ an excellent cook. He must be a man of taste and erudition and cultivate the society of writers, artists and scientists. He must be a naturally patient man, willing to spin out negotiations and to emulate the exquisite art of procrastination as perfected in the Vatican. He must be imperturbable, able to receive bad news without manifesting displeasure, or to hear himself maligned and misquoted without the slightest twinge of irritation. His private life must be so ascetic as to give his enemies no opportunity to spread scandal. He must be tolerant of the ignorance and foolishness of his home government and know how to temper the vehemence of the instructions he receives. Finally, he should remember that overt diplomatic triumphs leave feelings of humiliation behind them and a desire for revenge: no good negotiator should ever threaten, bully or chide.

Surely these are excellent precepts, which I should myself recommend to young diplomatists; although I might formulate them in rather different terms.

The diplomatic method exercised by sixteenth century Italians was less exemplary. Their ambassadors were generally furnished with two sets of instructions, the first being ostensible and the second secret. They were told to acclimatize themselves to local conditions and to assess how far it would be prudent for them to intervene in local political intrigues. Assassination, although occasionally resorted to by the envoys of Venice, was not thought to be the safest way of disposing of opponents: it was preferable to undermine their position by discrediting their motives: Louis XI of France was held up as a master in disseminating suspicion. Even more important was the art of acquiring influential friends: affability was not in itself sufficient for this purpose; it was essential to distribute bribes, subventions and other inducements with discrimination and tact. In the sixteenth century, as indeed in the two succeeding centuries, it was not regarded as in itself disgraceful that a statesman or courtier should receive monetary gifts from foreign Powers. Even the ladies of the Court, or the Cardinals of the Curia, expected to be offered presents by foreign ambassadors. Those rare eccentrics who refused bribes could be won over by other inducements such as titles, decorations, or heraldic, academic, or civic honours. Questionable though such practices were, there did exist a few rules of the game. It was illregarded to receive money for the purpose of actually betraying the interests of one's own country; and to accept a single payment, even of several thousand ducats, was thought more respectable than to be in receipt of a recurrent subvention or pension. Yet the fact that the Italian States did certainly advocate such methods renders it regrettable, as I have said, that modern diplomacy should have begun with them.

I must mention two diplomatic functions which were regarded as essential in the sixteenth century, and which have now either declined in importance or have wholly lapsed. In the days before newpapers existed and when foreign correspondents were unknown, an ambassador was regarded first and foremost as a source of news. The diplomatic archives of the time are bursting with complaints addressed by governments to their envoys for having failed to provide advance or detailed information, and of the pathetic excuses which the latter return. Thus in 1505 we find Mauroceno,

Venetian Ambassador to France, writing that it was all very well for the Signory to complain that he was never first with the news, since they themselves took no trouble to send him items of gossip that he could exchange for other information; and, if it comes to that, what about their never having sent him the falcons which he had promised as a present to Cardinal d'Amboise? 'You desert your orators,' Mauroceno, as many a subsequent ambassador, complains.

It was the overriding importance attached to the quick receipt of news, (a function performed today by the telegraph agencies and the newspapers), which, while it was the main cause of the establishment of permanent missions, also imposed upon envoys the dire necessity of constant presence at court. They were expected to attend the Sovereign to whom they were accredited, even when he was at his hunting lodge, even when he was on a campaign, even when he had retired to some villa, even when he was ill in bed. This necessity was a torture to ambassadors, keeping them for ever on the jump, exposing them to long days on horseback and nights in abominable inns, even as it was an intolerable imposition upon Kings and Ministers. The monarchs of the period devoted much ingenuity to outwitting questing diplomatists and amused themselves by exposing them to unnecessary exertions and displacements. These functions in the modern world are fulfilled by newspaper reporters, who are usually younger and more adventurous men. All the ambassador need do is to comment, in the quiet of his own study, upon the news they send.

5

The three volumes of Monsieur de Maulde-la-Clavière's massive work on '*La Diplomatie au temps de Machiavel*' constitute a quarry, from which great blocks of information, together with a whole pebble-beach of instances, can be derived. We learn from him how widely and immediately the art of negotiation, as evolved among the Italian States of the Renaissance, was copied by other foreign Courts; and to what extent modern diplomatic theory and practice derive from that unfortunate tradition. I shall examine the method of negotiation that developed during the fifteenth and sixteenth centuries under three headings, namely, the negotiation of treaties, the system of diplomacy by conference, and the undue but inevitable importance then attached to questions of precedence.

The negotiation of treaties, during the fifteenth century at least, was complicated by the survival of feudal traditions and the conception of papal supremacy. A suzerain might claim that some small State was in law his vassal and had thus no '*droit d'ambassade*', or no right to conclude treaties with other States without his approval. Thus the King of France contended that Navarre, Béarn and the county of Foix could not form the subject of negotiation between other States, since they must be regarded as pertaining to the internal or domestic policies of the French Court. The Pope, for his part, sometimes claimed the right of intervention on the principle '*ad Papam pertinet pacem facere inter principes christianos*'. Analogous situations arise today when a country claims that a given dispute, affecting, let us say, the rights of Cyprus or Morocco, pertains to the domestic policy of the suzerain State and are not therefore fit subjects for international discussion.

In spite of these difficulties, negotiations were frequent and treaties assumed elaborate forms. Apart from regular treaties in our sense of the term, there were 'protocols of agreement', containing a list of points accepted, but often not signed by the contracting parties. There were also 'endentures' namely documents cut in zigzag shape into two pieces, each side retaining one of the two sundered halves. In addition to this there was a form of validation of a treaty by the papal notaries, which was regarded as the most binding, the *validissima et amplissima* form of treaty and which the French referred to as an *acte authentique*. It was the Pope alone who could release Princes from their oaths, or who could excommunicate those of them who broke engagements solemnly authenticated by the Vatican notary. Thus we find a Treaty between Louis XI and the Duke of Brittany containing a clause under which both Princes explicitly undertook not to solicit the Pope to release them from the oaths exchanged.

Ratification of treaties assumed the most ceremonial form. They were huge sheets of parchment containing, not the terms of the treaty only, not merely the full powers given to the negotiating ambassadors, but also long gnomic passages about peace, justice and virtue. It was taken for granted that a Sovereign could not refuse to ratify a treaty negotiated by an ambassador possessing full powers, unless it could be shown that he had flagrantly exceeded his instructions. Both Guicciardini and Machiavelli express horror at the action of Ferdinand and Isabella in refusing to ratify a treaty negotiated and signed with France by Spanish ambassadors bearing full powers. Such repudiation, they rightly suggested, would, if it became a habit, render impossible all sound negotiation between States. It would have seemed inconceivable to them, for instance, that in the year 1919 the United States legislature should have repudiated a treaty negotiated and signed by the President in person. They would have found it difficult to understand the mysteries of the American Constitution.

In addition to political treaties, there were all manner of commercial treaties, called *'actes d'entrecours'*, which provided, often in great detail, for mutual trade and establishment. A good specimen of such treaties was the Treaty of Commerce concluded between England and Florence in 1490. Under this treaty England undertook to give Florence a monopoly of the wool trade in Italy, while Florence undertook to allow the English merchants to establish themselves as a corporation in Pisa, under their own consul. Disputes between a Pisan citizen and a British merchant, would be tried by a mixed tribunal composed of the Consul and the Podestà. Thus we see the old Greek idea of a Proxenos developing into that of a *baglio*, or consul, generally appointed, and paid for, by the local merchants of his own nation, and exercising certain judicial functions such as later developed into the capitulations, as established until recent times in the Levant and the Far East. There also existed, until late in the sixteenth century, a system by which a merchant who was owed money by a foreign merchant could obtain a 'letter of reprisal', which entitled him to seize property in his own country belonging to a merchant from the country in which he had been injured. Thus an English merchant unable to recover a debt from a Genoese merchant had the right to distrain upon Genoese property in London or Bristol. This system led to much injustice and bitterness: its abolition is praised by such an authority as M. de Maulde-la-Clavière as 'the greatest triumph that diplomacy can record in the course of centuries'. There were other tentative attempts made to mitigate the chaotic misfortunes to which international commerce was exposed, including some rudimentary provisions, such as the Venetian 'Consolato del Mare', or the 'Tables of Amalfi', to regulate maritime law between trading nations. Such provisions and institutions were assuredly an advance on the older systems of piracy.

Even in the fifteenth century, professional diplomatists regarded with grave doubts the method now known as 'Diplomacy by Conference', which in those days took the form of personal interviews between sovereigns. There was always the danger that one monarch might kidnap the other monarch and for this reason the interviews generally took place in the centre of a bridge, when the two sovereigns could exchange compliments through a stout oaken lattice erected between them. This strange device was revived by Napoleon in 1807 when he held a conference with Alexander I on a barge moored in the middle of the Memel river. There were other disadvantages inherent in such personal interviews. They were enormously expensive, since each side competed with the other in ostentation; they aroused exaggerated expectations at home and deep suspicion abroad; they raised a wild covey of disturbing rumours; and, since such agreement as might be reached was verbal and not written, opportunities were open for subsequent misunderstanding and prevarication. Moreover there was always the danger that the two sovereigns, who were unaccustomed to conversing with equals, and who probably knew not one word of each other's language, would return from the interview not in amity, but with sentiments of lasting personal dislike. Edward IV spoke excellent French, but his interview with Louis XI through a lattice on a bridge across the Somme, when seven thousand English soldiers were strewn dead drunk through the streets of Amiens, produced no diplomatic result of value. And when the same astute French King met the King of Castille on a bridge across the Bidassoa in 1462, he never recovered from the unpleasantness of that brief but harsh encounter. It is not surprising that Philippe de Comines, an experienced if corrupt diplomatist of the time, should have recorded the following opinion of Diplomacy by Conference: 'Two great Princes, who wish to establish good personal relations should never meet each other face to face, but ought to communicate through good and wise ambassadors.'

Another disadvantage bequeathed by the diplomatic method of the Renaissance was the enormous importance attached to questions of ceremonial. An ambassador, on arrival, had often to negotiate for weeks every detail of his official reception and the presentation of his letters of credence. Should the King actually descend the steps of the throne to receive the letters, or should he make a mere movement of the legs only, indicative of his theoretical willingness so to do? At what exact stage in the proceedings should the ambassador remove or replace his hat? Would an occasion occur when the King would invite the ambassador, if only for a moment, to sit upon a stool? If the ambassador delivered his formal address in Latin, as was then customary, would the King reply in the same language, or use his own vernacular, or not reply at all? Such matters, unimportant though they appear to us, formed the subject of long interviews and interminable despatches.

The problem of precedence was even more serious. The original theory was that ambassadors ranked according to the antiquity of the States they represented. In 1504 Pope Julius II had composed a table of precedence, under which the Emperor came first, the King of France second, the King of Spain third, and so on down to the smaller dukes, despots and princes. Under this table the King of England came seventh on the list, after the King of Portugal but just in front of the King of Sicily. It was inevitable that, with the decline of papal authority, the fluctuations in comparative power, and the rise of new and highly self-assertive national monarchies, this original class-list should have been disputed. The Spaniards, for instance, never accepted the ruling that their ambassadors should rank after those of the King of France. The serenity of Courts, the actual progress of negotiations or the signature of treaties, were disturbed and embarrassed by this eternal controversy. Ungainly incidents were always occurring, one of the most notorious of which took place in London in 1661, when the coach of the Spanish ambassador tried to push in front of that of the French ambassador, a battle occurred with loss of life among the footmen and postilions, diplomatic relations were severed between Paris and Madrid and a very real danger of war arose. As late as 1768, at a Court Ball in London, the French Ambassador, observing that the Russian Ambassador had established himself in a front seat next to the Austrian Ambassador, climbed round over the back benches and inserted himself physically between them. This led to a duel at which the Russian Ambassador was severely wounded. This sensitiveness in regard to precedence also complicated the signature of international treaties, since each representative asserted that the dignity of his master would be offended if he signed his name below that of any other repre-sentive. For a certain period, this difficulty was met by the absurd device of signing treaties in circular form, like a round robin, thus giving no single signatory definite pride of place. The awkwardness of this method led to the adoption of the system called the *'alternat'*, by which several copies of the same treaty were prepared and each plenipotentiary signed his own copy first. This system entailed much unnecessary labour and delay. It seems strange to us that it was not until 1815 that the statesmen of Europe realised that this ridicu-lous problem of precedence bequeathed to them by the Middle Ages was wholly intolerable. The *Règlement* of the Vienna Congress established four classes of diplo-matic representatives, namely Ambassadors and papal legates, Ministers plenipotentiary, Ministers Resident, and Chargés d'Affaires. Precedence within these four categories was in future to be regulated according to the date at which an envoy had presented his letters of credence. The Senior Ambassador, namely the one who had been longest at the post, was to be styled the Dean, or *Doyen*, of the Diplomatic Body. At the Congress of

Aix-la-Chapelle, held three years later, it was further decided that treaties should be signed in the alphabetical order of the contracting States. These excellent rules settled the problem of precedence for more than a hundred years.

The time may now have come when they might with advantage be brought up to date. The flocks of Ambassadors who congregate like starlings around the capitals today, might well be divided by international agreement into categories according to the power and responsibilities of the nations they represent. And the old alphabetical order, which was based on the French alphabet, might also be revised, since it still remains uncertain whether the United States of America should figure under A. or E. or U., whether the United Kingdom should figure under R. or E. or B., and whether Russia should figure under U. or S. or R. These problems, however, are not comparable to the excruciating controversies aroused by precedence up to the early nineteenth century; and these controversies were the direct inheritance of the confused and highly competitive diplomatic method bequeathed to us by the Italian Renaissance.

Their methods were unsound both in theory and practice. In teaching men that international justice must always be subordinated to national expediency, in inculcating the habits of deception, opportunism, and faithlessness, the Italians did much to bring the whole art of diplomacy into disrepute. In their desire to obtain immediate results in precarious situations, they indulged in transitory '*combinazioni*' and ignored what might be called the 'gradualness' of good negotiation. It was for the statesmen of the seventeenth and eighteenth centuries to develop a more sensible and thus a more reliable diplomatic method. In my next lecture I shall examine the improvements that were then introduced.

# III

## THE FRENCH SYSTEM

I

In my last lecture I said that diplomacy has suffered much from the false values bequeathed by Byzantium to the Italians of the Renaissance. I suggested that the unreliability of their method, with its attendant blemishes of stratagem and suspicion, was due mainly to the impermanence of their systems; and that the vacuum left by the decline in papal and imperial authority, had been filled by an excitable scramble for power and by a succession of fluctuating combinations. These chaotic practices were brought to an end, largely owing to the influence and power of two remarkable men, a great international jurist and a great national statesman; Grotius and Richelieu.

Hugo Grotius of Delft was a rare infant prodigy, in that he remained prodigious until his death at the age of sixty-two. When he was still a child he wrote Latin hexameters of exquisite purity and precision and edited the work of the Carthaginian lawyer, Martianus Capella: at the age of fifteen he served as a very young diplomatist under Count Justin of Nassau on an embassy to the court of France; by the time he was seventeen he had written three plays in Latin which were admired far beyond the circle of Dutch humanists; at the age of twenty he was appointed official historiographer to the States General, and at the age of twenty-one he had already completed the first draft of his great work, the *De jure belli et pacis*.

I am not concerned with Grotius the jurist, or with his creative influence on the development of international law. I am concerned with his contribution to the general theory of diplomacy and with the precepts that he advocated for the better conduct of international relations. From this aspect it may be said that Grotius was the only begetter of four important principles.

In an age of acute religious conflict, he asserted that there was no sense at all in Catholics and Protestants seeking to impose their special dogmas upon each other; and that, if only they would *think* quietly, instead of *feeling* wildly, humanity would be relieved of much meaningless wastage and much atrocious suffering.

He asserted that, above all doctrinal animosities, above all dynastic or national ambitions, there existed a Law of Nature, evolved, as it were organically, from the conscience and reason of mankind. It was this law which was the ordained successor to the ancient disciplines of Pope and Emperor. It was independent of Kings or Governments or Institutions; it was more ancient than these, and far more durable, since it derived from the rational in man. Unless humanity recognised and accepted the Law of Nature, there could be nothing to prevent a continuance of international anarchy.

He asserted that, without general obedience to this

Law of Nature, the theory of the balance of power would prove a dangerous rather than a tutelary principle. No just equilibrium could ever be secured unless the rulers of the world realised that there were certain principles other than national expediency that must govern their policies and their acts.

In the fourth place, Grotius was the first systematic philosopher to propose that some institution should be established whereby the Law of Nature could be administered and enforced. His idea was that the Christian Powers, whether Catholic or Protestant, should create 'some kind of body, in whose assemblies the quarrels of each one might be terminated by the judgement of others not interested'. He realised that such a body would be nothing more than a deliberative assembly unless it were given the power to impose sanctions. He suggested therefore that 'means be sought to constrain the parties to agree to reasonable conditions'.

Such principles, such recommendations, were far in advance of the general climate of opinion of the year 1625. It is not surprising that Grotius should have been imprisoned in a fortress and should, after his dramatic escape, have died in exile, shipwrecked amid the sands and conifers of the lone Baltic Sea.

Hugo Grotius was an idealist. Almost three centuries were destined to pass, and many wars to be endured, before any statesman attempted to put his ideas into practice. Yet his contemporary, Cardinal Richelieu, who was before anything a realist, did succeed, during his own lifetime, in introducing certain reforms both in the theory and practice of diplomatic method.

Richelieu was the first to establish that the art of

negotiation must be a permanent activity and not merely a hurried endeavour. In his Political Testament he stated it as a principle that diplomacy should aim, not at incidental or opportunist arrangements, but at creating solid and durable relations. Even a negotiation that failed was not a wasted effort, since it would always serve as a means of acquiring experience and knowledge. It was thus Richelieu who first laid it down as a definite precept that diplomacy was not a mere *ad hoc* operation but a continuous process. This, surely, was an important concept to have originated.

In the second place Richelieu taught his contemporaries that the interest of the State was primary and eternal; that it was above sentimental, ideological or doctrinal prejudices and affections. If national interest demanded an alliance with an obnoxious, even with a heretic, State, then no feelings of what one liked or what one disliked should be permitted to blur that necessity. In moments of danger one should choose one's allies, not for their integrity or charm, but for their physical or even geographical value.

In an age of undisputed autocracy, Richelieu was original also in contending that no policy could succeed unless it had national opinion behind it. However secretive may have been the methods practised by himself and Father Joseph, he did realise that some steps should be taken to inform, and above all to instruct, those who influenced the thoughts and feelings of the people as a whole. He was the first to introduce a system of domestic propaganda; the pamphlets which he caused to be written and circulated (what he called '*mes petits écrits*', 'my little leaflets') were designed to create a body of informed opinion favourable to his policies. I suppose that was an advance in diplomatic method: let us at least call it an advance.

The Cardinal again inculcated into all his ambassadors and subordinates the important doctrine that a treaty is a most serious instrument and one to be entered into only with the utmost caution. Once a treaty has been negotiated, signed and ratified, it must be observed, (and I am quoting Richelieu's actual words) 'with religious scruple.' He insisted that ambassadors and negotiators should in no circumstances be permitted to exceed their instructions, since by so doing they might compromise the good faith of their sovereign. I am not suggesting that this principle was invariably observed by French diplomacy of the seventeenth century. I am merely saying that the greatest diplomatist of the age insisted upon that principle for purposes that were not ethical only, but also practical.

Richelieu's influence on contemporary diplomatic thought and practice was determinant. The example that he set, the lessons that he inculcated, were not always exemplary. But he did establish the important principle that the most essential of all the components of sound diplomacy was the element of certainty. It was not only that negotiation must result in agreements, the wording of which was so precise as to leave no scope for future evasions or misunderstandings: it was also that each party to a negotiation should know from the outset that the other party really represented the sovereign authority in his own country. Unless some certainty existed that an agreement once signed would be ratified and executed, then the give and take of negotiation became impossible, and international con-

ferences degenerated into assemblies for the exchange of
entertainment, platitudes or propaganda.

Richelieu saw therefore that negotiation would always be ineffective unless the direction of policy and
the control of ambassadors were concentrated in a
single Ministry. He saw that any dispersal of responsibility would merely bewilder both his own ambassadors and those with whom they might negotiate.
Until his day several different Ministries felt they had
the right to dabble in foreign policy and to receive
reports from French ambassadors abroad. By the
Decree of March 11, 1626 Richelieu concentrated all
responsibility within the Ministry of External Affairs,
over which he himself maintained constant super-
vision. He thereby secured that the word of command
in foreign affairs should be delivered by a single voice
only, and not by a chorus of discordant voices. This
useful principle of centralization of responsibility was
not always observed by his successors. It appears to be
almost unrealised in modern times.

2

I have entitled this, my third lecture 'The French
System', since, even as it was the Italians who set the
diplomatic tone for the fifteenth and sixteenth centuries, so also it was the French who, in the two centuries that followed, established the pattern that was
imitated by all other European States. Since it was
during the reign of Louis XIV that French influence on
diplomatic method became predominant and universal,
it is necessary to examine in some detail the machinery
which during those seventy years was devised and to
some extent perfected.

Under Louis XIV the Secretary of State for Foreign Affairs was a permanent member of the Cabinet, or Conseil d'Etat; he was nominated by the King, generally because of his previous diplomatic experience, and held his appointment at the King's pleasure. He would often find his province encroached upon by the Minister of Finance, even as Foreign Secretaries in our own time have sometimes found the Prime Minister, or Chancellor of the Exchequer, taking too close an interest in the affairs of the Foreign Office. It was the Secretary of State who, in theory at least, received foreign ambassadors in Paris and gave instructions to the French ambassadors abroad. But sometimes the King himself would receive foreign ambassadors without his Foreign Secretary being present at the audience, and often the King would write to French ambassadors abroad and fail to inform the Secretary of State of what he had said. Louis XIV, although autocratic, was not inconsiderate to the Ministers he employed. Although it was he who fixed the agenda for Cabinet Meetings and always had the last word, he would listen patiently and receive opinions, and even criticisms, with grace. Before giving audiences to foreign ambassadors he was always careful to obtain in advance a memorandum from the Foreign Office advising him what subjects to avoid. He was on such occasions both discreet and tactful, nor is there any recorded instance of his having committed his Foreign Secretary to any impossible courses or pledges. Yet even Louis XIV would occasionally conduct secret negotiations behind the back of the Minister responsible, although these were generally confined to family and dynastic matters. It was in subsequent reigns that the '*secret du roi*' and the '*secret de l'empereur*' caused such sad havoc in French diplomacy.

Under the Secretary of State was a small Foreign Office, consisting of a few clerks, translators and cypher officers, nominated by the Secretary of State personally, and liable to lose their posts when their patron died or fell from favour. In the memoirs of Brienne we are told that, one day in 1661, the whole Foreign Office was summoned in a body to Vincennes. Brienne the elder went there in a sedan chair; Brienne the younger went in a carriage accompanied by the two senior clerks or *commis*; the two junior clerks went on horseback, carrying with them ink and paper in case of need. It requires no great mathematical powers to deduce from this account that the Quai d'Orsay of those days consisted of five officials.

The French Diplomatic Service, on the other hand, was more extensive than that of any other Power. By 1685 the French possessed permanent embassies in Rome, Venice, Constantinople, Vienna, the Hague, London, Madrid, Lisbon, Munich, Copenhagen and Berne; there were special missions to Würtemberg, the Elector Palatine and the Elector of Mainz. Ministers Resident were established at Mantua, Genoa, Hamburg, Geneva and Florence. These numerous envoys were classified under the categories of Ambassadors Extraordinary, Ambassadors Ordinary, Envoys and Residents. In later years it was regarded as humiliating to be dubbed just 'ordinary' and all Ambassadors were accorded the title of 'extraordinary' even when that epithet had lost its meaning. Louis XIV was not in favour of employing ecclesiastics in his diplomatic service, since he felt they might be too much under the influence of the Vatican. Yet the old difficulty arose that prominent people did not relish being sent on embassies abroad because of the exile and the expense involved. It thus became a frequent practice to choose ambassadors, not from the ranks of the old court nobility, but from among the *gens de robe*. The idea grew up that nobles of ancient family must be sent to Rome, Madrid, Vienna and London, whereas officials would do well enough for Switzerland, Holland and Venice. Ambassadors, unless they were flagrantly incompetent or contradictory, retained their appointments for at least three or four years; in the event of the death of their own sovereign or of the sovereign to whom they were accredited new letters of credence had to be issued. If war was declared while an ambassador was still at his post he was exposed to great inconvenience before transport could be arranged; his baggage was almost invariably looted before he reached his home.

During the long period when France remained the model of diplomatic method great importance was attached to the written 'Instructions' with which an ambassador was provided before leaving for his post. These documents, which were composed in the most careful manner, contained not only a statement of the policy to be pursued by the ambassador, but a full account of political conditions in the country to which he was accredited. Delicate and often waspish comments were added on the origins, careers and characters of those statesmen and diplomatic colleagues with whom he would have to negotiate. A minister such as Vergennes would devote hours of blissful energy to the composition of these 'Instructions' which to this day remain models of classic prose. As the years passed and French Ministers became more and more intoxicated by the wine of logical expression, these Instructions developed into literary exercises of the utmost elegance. In 1774, for instance, the 'Memorandum of Instructions issued to Sieur Baron de Breteuil, about to reside in Vienna with the quality of Ambassador Extraordinary' is a whole volume, divided into five separate chapters, covering the entire European situation and indicating the policy to be pursued, not towards Austria only, but in every continental country. These instructions, moreover, contained certain stock paragraphs, expressive of the highest religious and moral sentiments, and urging the Ambassador in his despatches 'to add nothing to the truth'.

The French diplomatic tradition has always attached importance to style. To this day the despatches and Notes of French Ambassadors are superior in their lucidity and concision to those of any other diplomatist. The French language again, which during the seventeenth and eighteenth centuries became the *lingua franca* of diplomacy, is better adapted than any other to an intercourse requiring the perfect fusion of courtesy with precision. Yet it is perhaps dangerous for government officials to become too sensitive to the charms of literary composition, since it may lead them and their employers to suppose that an opinion neatly or beautifully expressed must also be accurate and wise. In our own Foreign Service, fortunately, the man of letters has always been regarded with bewildered, although quite friendly, disdain.

The instructions with which a French Ambassador was furnished also contained definite orders regarding the points of etiquette, precedence and ceremonial on which he must insist and indications as to the sort of people whose acquaintance should be cultivated. Thus in the instruction handed in 1712 to the duc d'Aumont on his appointment as Ambassador to London we find the sentence: 'The English Constitution is such that it is not regarded as offensive by the Court of St. James for ambassadors to have relations with the opposition. The duc d'Aumont need not, therefore, reject the society of the Whigs.'

The Instruction often enclosed the official letter of credence together with certain letters of introduction to prominent people signed by the Secretary of State. Two cyphers were also enclosed, one for ordinary correspondence and one for highly secret correspondence. The ambassador was instructed to preserve the latter carefully in his private *'casette'* or safe.

The staffs of the Embassies were selected and paid for by the Ambassador himself. His secretaries and attachés were chosen from the circle of his own family and friends and were often wholly unfitted to their functions. In 1712 M. de Torcy, regretting the amateurishness of the French foreign service, set up a small Political Academy for the training of six young diplomatists who were called 'les Messieurs du Cabinet'. This experiment was not successful and lasted but six years. For purposes of personal and national prestige the staffs that ambassadors were supposed to take with them were both otiose and extravagant. Thus Pierre de Girardin who went as Ambassador to Constantinople in 1686 took with him 'fifteen gentlemen', two secretaries, a lady in waiting for his wife, a steward, and as many as 60 servants including ten musicians. They had to bring with them all their own furniture, pictures, plate and tapestry and were obliged on arrival to hire an Embassy house at their own expense. Thus encumbered, their progress to their post was dangerous and slow. It took one French Ambassador two and a half months of continuous travel to get from Paris to Stockholm. We can understand that the honour of being appointed ambassador to a distant post was not accepted with any enthusiasm and that the King in many cases had to bring formidable pressure to bear.

It was inevitable that in a system for so long dominated by the powerful personality of Colbert a new importance should be attached to economic matters. Ambassadors were instructed to do everything within their power to foster French commerce. The Levant trade was regarded as of such special value that the ambassador to the Porte was often appointed, not by the Foreign Secretary, but by the Minister of Finance and Trade. He was expected, before leaving France, to consult with the Chamber of Commerce at Marseilles and to pay full attention to their demands and recommendations. Moreover something like a Levant Consular Service was set up as early as the seventeenth century with a body of student interpreters called '*les jeunes des langues*'. The French Consuls in the Levant addressed their reports, not to the Foreign Ministry, but to the Admiralty: they were placed in charge of the French trade depots or *scalas* throughout the Levant and became people of considerable political influence and power.

So much for the French foreign service abroad during the seventeenth century. It remains to consider the treatment accorded to foreign diplomatists in Paris and the method of negotiating treaties.

Curious as it may appear to us, it was not the custom in the seventeenth century to obtain the previous consent or *agrément* of a foreign monarch or government before despatching an ambassador. The name of the *nuncio* whom the Pope wished to send to Paris was, it is true, submitted in advance for the approval of Louis XIV. In other cases the man just seems to have turned up. Thus when in 1685 Sir William Trumbull, who as we know from Pepys was not in any company a *persona grata*, arrived in Paris with full credentials as British Ambassador, Louis XIV was much annoyed. This great monarch moreover had the habit of marking his personal likes or dislikes for an ambassador or his sovereign by the quality of the reception accorded and by the ceremonial observed. It is true that even at that date there existed an official corresponding to the Marshal of the Diplomatic Corps, but the most careful plans that the *Introducteur des Ambassadeurs* might arrange in advance were apt to be disorganised at the last moment by the sovereign himself. Eventually the details of the official entry and reception would be arranged, the ambassador and his staff would for the moment be lodged in the 'Hôtel des Ambassadeurs' in the Rue de Tournon, and the official visits would be paid. But foreign ambassadors were not admitted to the daily ceremonies of Versailles, they were lucky if they could catch the monarch as he left Mass on Sundays, and they were accorded no reserved seats at Court banquets or concerts. When one evening in 1698 the King asked the Earl of Portland to hold his bedroom candlestick, the episode resounded through the chancelleries of Europe as a highly significant, and perhaps portentous, event.

Louis XIV, being a man of intelligence and reflection, did not at all approve of diplomacy by conference. He felt that this was a slow, expensive and cumbrous method of negotiation, and preferred confidential discussions between experts. 'Open negotiations,' he wrote, 'incline negotiators to consider their own prestige and to maintain the dignity, the interests and the arguments of their sovereigns with undue obstinacy and prevent them from giving way to the frequently superior arguments of the occasion.' By this he meant of course that it is far easier to make concessions in private discussion than when many observers are present round the table. Louis XIV was certainly of opinion that international relations are less likely to become tense or embittered if they are handled by a few professionals; thus although he permitted the Parlement of Paris and the local Parlements to publish and register the treaties he concluded, he regarded this process as, so to speak, notarial only, and would have been deeply shocked if any member of any Parlement had ventured to express any opinion at all. His abiding principle was that negotiation must remain as confidential as possible. There have been worse diplomatic principles.

3

I am not suggesting that the foreign policy pursued by Louis XIV from the death of Mazarin in 1661 to the Treaty of Utrecht in 1713, should serve as an example to future statesmen. It was governed by principles and ambitions of which historians have disapproved. All I am saying is that, from the advent of Richelieu to power in 1616 until the Revolution more than a hundred and sixty years later, the diplomatic method of France became the model for all Europe: and that, given the ideas and circumstances of the time, it was an excellent method.

From his experience of that system, François de Callières wrote his great work '*De la manière de négociér avec les Souverains*', which was first published in 1716, and which remains to this day the best manual of diplomatic method ever written. I shall examine it in some detail.

François de Callières, who was born at Thorigny in 1645, was the son of one of Louis XIV's generals and served, first as a secret agent and then as an accredited envoy, in the Netherlands, Germany and Poland. As Minister Plenipotentiary he represented France at the discussions that led to the Treaty of Ryswick. He was thereafter appointed Secretary to the Cabinet, or Conseil d'Etat. He was thus a man of long practical experience and his reflections on the art of negotiation deserve respectful attention.

De Callières entirely disagreed with the theory that the purpose of diplomacy is to deceive. On the contrary, he contended that sound diplomacy is based on the creation of confidence and that confidence can be inspired only by good faith. Let me summarize some of the relevant passages from his great book:

> 'A diplomatist,' he writes, 'should remember that open dealing is the basis of confidence; he should share freely with others everything except what it is his duty to conceal. ... A good negotiator will never rely for the success of his mission either on bad faith or on promises

that he cannot execute. It is a fundamental error, and one widely held, that a clever negotiator must be a master of deceit. Deceit is indeed the measure of the smallness of mind of him who uses it; it proves that he does not possess sufficient intelligence to achieve results by just and reasonable means. Honesty is here and everywhere the best policy; a lie always leaves behind it a drop of poison and even the most brilliant diplomatic success gained by trickery rests on an insecure foundation, since it awakes in the defeated party a sense of irritation, a desire for vengeance, and a hatred which must remain a menace to his foe. . . . The use of deceit in diplomacy is by its very nature limited, since there is no curse that comes quicker to roost than a lie that has been found out. Apart from the fact that a lie is unworthy of a great Ambassador, it actually does more harm than good to negotiation, since though it may confer success today, it will create an atmosphere of suspicion which tomorrow will make further success impossible. . . . The negotiator therefore must be a man of probity and one who loves truth: otherwise he will fail to inspire confidence.'

To Callières good diplomatic method was akin to good banking, being founded upon the establishment of credit. 'The secret of negotiation,' he writes, 'is to harmonize the real interests of the parties concerned.' There must be no menaces or bullying even as there must be no deception; the expression 'diplomatic triumph' is one that should never be used. Let me quote his wise words again:

'Menaces always do harm to negotiation, since they often push a party to extremes to which they would not have resorted but for provocation. It is well known that hurt vanity often goads men to courses which a sober estimate of their own interests would lead them to eschew. . . . Success achieved by force or fraud rests on an insecure foundation; conversly, success based on reciprocal advantage gives promise of even further successes to come. An ambassador must base his success on straightforward and honest procedure, if he tries to win by subtlety or arrogance he is deceiving himself.'

Apart from establishing these excellent principles of negotiation, de Callières has much that is most important to say about the specific qualities that a diplomatist ought to possess. I shall summarize his catalogue, using his own words:

'The good diplomatist,' he writes, 'must have an observant mind, a gift of application which rejects being diverted by pleasures or frivolous amusements, a sound judgement which takes the measure of things as they are, and which goes straight to the goal by the shortest and most natural paths without wandering into meaningless refinements and subtleties.

The good negotiator must have the gift of penetration such as will enable him to discern the thoughts of men and to deduce from the least movement of their features which passions are stirring within.

The diplomatist must be quick, resourceful, a good listener, courteous and agreeable. He should not seek to gain a reputation as a wit, nor should he be so disputatious as to divulge secret information in order to clinch an argument. Above all the good negotiator must possess enough self-control to resist the longing to speak before he has thought out what he intends to say. He must not fall into the mistake of supposing that an air of mystery, in which secrets are made out of nothing and the merest trifle exalted into an affair of State, is anything but the symptom of a small mind. He should pay attention to women, but never lose his heart. He must be able to simulate dignity even if he does not possess it, but he must at the same time avoid all tasteless display. Courage also is an essential quality, since no timid man can hope to bring a confidential negotiation to success. The negotiator must possess the patience of a watch-maker and be devoid of personal prejudices. He must have a calm nature, be able to suffer fools gladly, and should not be given to drink, gambling, women, irritability, or any other wayward humours and fantasies. The negotiator moreover should study history and memoirs, be acquainted with foreign institutions and habits, and be able to tell where, in any foreign country, the real sovereignty lies. Everyone who enters the profession of diplomacy should know the German, Italian and Spanish languages as well as the Latin, ignorance of which would be a disgrace and shame to any public man, since it is the common language of all Christian nations. He should also have some knowledge of literature, science, mathematics, and law. Finally he should entertain handsomely. A good cook is often an excellent conciliator.'

This assuredly is a formidable catalogue of qualifications and capacities. You will have observed that the gift of rhetoric does not figure among the many talents with which the ideal diplomatist should be endowed. The old conception of an ambassador as an advocate or orator had by then wholly disappeared. It was not until the democratic method of diplomacy was revived in the twentieth century that forensic ability again resumed its clumsy place among the arts of negotiation.

Having devoted much space to the mental and moral equipment of the ideal negotiator, Callières proceeds to consider the machinery of negotiation. He divides diplomatists into four main categories, namely ambassadors, envoys, residents and deputies or commissars. An ambassador represents his sovereign and is entitled to special privileges, such as remaining covered in the royal presence and driving his coach into the inner courtyard of the Louvre. Envoys represent their governments rather than their sovereigns and are therefore obliged to uncover in the King's presence and do not make a state entry into the capital. Ministers resident were regarded by Callières as inferior creatures, whereas the Deputies or Commissars who represented free cities such as Hamburg or Lübeck ought not to be accorded diplomatic privileges, being little more than the agents of trading corporations. It is curious to find a man as sensible as Callières still claiming that the French Ambassadors should 'as an immemorial right' have precedence over the ambassadors of other States, including Austria. It is rare that we find him being pedantic or old-fashioned.

Callières, as is the way with those who have served for long in any profession, was distrustful of amateurs. A wise sovereign, he says, should recruit and train a professional diplomatic service, being careful to see that the young attachés are chosen for their merit rather than for their family connections. 'Nepotism,' he writes, 'is the veritable curse of the service.' Ecclesiastics should not, in his opinion, be included in the profession, since they cannot be sent to infidel courts, and ought not to be sent to Rome. Soldiers do not make good diplomatists, since an ambassador should be a man of peace. The legal mind, he asserts, is not adapted to diplomacy, 'In general,' he writes, 'the training of a lawyer breeds habits and dispositions of mind which are not favourable to the practice of diplomacy.' Few persons who have had experience of lawyer-diplomatists will deny the truth of this assertion.

Thus equipped and thus selected the Ambassador

proceeds to his post. The first essential of course is that
he should possess the full confidence of his own home
government; the most perfect ambassador is valueless
unless his advice carries weight with his own Sovereign
or Minister, and unless they in their turn disclose to
him the full nature of their policies and desires. In the
second place the ambassador must render himself liked
and trusted in the country where he resides; not only
must he by his honesty gain the confidence of official
circles, but he must render himself agreeable to society
as a whole. With this in mind he must praise rather than
criticize local conditions and must give the impression
that he enjoys the life he leads. He will find it profitable carefully to study the history, art and literature
of the country in which he resides, indicating thereby
that he, as a foreigner, even as a Frenchman, has much
to learn from their own form of culture. He should
know how to distribute bribes and subventions with
discretion and tact. He will often find that it is valuable
to pay money to such minor characters as ballet
dancers or orderly officers, who have access to cabinets
and Princes, and who are generally in debt. Yet an
Ambassador should never personally dispense the
secret service funds at his disposal: he should leave all
this side of his work to the junior members of his staff,
who should have acquaintances in every camp and in
every grade of society. The ambassador himself should
never indulge in espionage or secret undertakings, nor,
except perhaps in England and Holland, should he
consort with members of the opposition. Finally an
ambassador should realize that there exists such a thing
as the freemasonry of the diplomatic corps and should
be careful to cultivate the friendship of even his minor

colleagues. 'An Ambassador,' writes de Callières, 'may very probably find that his colleagues of the diplomatic corps in the capital where he resides may be of value to him. Since the whole diplomatic body labours to the same end, namely to discover what is happening, there arises a certain freemasonry of diplomacy, by which one colleague informs another of coming events which a lucky chance has enabled him to discern.'

Finally de Callières raises the question that has so often faced honourable diplomatists with a moral problem, namely the question whether they were ever justified in refusing to execute the instructions they received from their own government. He implies, although he does not say so explicitly, that a diplomatist should always carry out the instructions that he receives from his Sovereign or his Minister, since, whereas they have before them the whole pattern of policy, he can only know the conditions existing at his own post at the time. But de Callières does make one notable exception. An ambassador should refuse to obey instructions when they entail doing something 'against the laws of God or of Justice'. He should thus refuse to instigate assassination or even to use his diplomatic immunity to foment or protect revolutionaries intriguing against the Sovereign to whom he is accredited.

Such therefore are the principles and precepts recommended, so long ago as 1716, by François de Callières. I have dealt with them at length since no other writer, not even Cambon or Jusserand, has given so clear, so complete, or so unanswerable a definition of good diplomatic method.

### 4

The ideals advocated by Callières were not maintained in the years that followed. In his early manhood the principle of the Balance of Power represented an equilibrium, which might well have been rendered a just equilibrium, between the strength of the Austrian Empire and the strength of France. He lived to see the emergence of three new Great Powers. England, Russia and Prussia. It was Frederick the Great who revived the old Italian theory of transitory combinations for immediate ends. Yet the lasting damage which this great soldier did to diplomatic theory and method was that he discredited the excellent system of the Balance of Power. Until then, in theory at least, that system had been essentially defensive, seeking to render it dangerous for any single Power to aim at dominating Europe or suppressing the liberties of others. Frederick the Great rendered it an aggressive system, a conspiracy for loot, by which the strong could obtain simultaneous accessions of territory at the expense of the weak. The successive partitions of Poland were not merely unjust in themselves, but they also did lasting damage to the principle of the Balance of Power. It required almost half a century and a series of terrible wars before the statesmen of the Congress of Vienna were able to re-establish the Balance of Power as a creditable principle of foreign policy and to found a system that preserved the world from major war for exactly one hundred years.

There were other important changes that Callières witnessed before his death in 1717. The Treaty of Utrecht gave international recognition to our own

Revolution of 1688, thereby marking the end of the old theory that the interests, even the personal and family interests, of princes were identical with those of their peoples. Sovereigns who desired for personal reasons to conduct a foreign policy not acceptable to their own peoples, were obliged to do so privately and by underhand means. This led, in the course of the eighteenth century, to an increase in the distracting habit of conducting a dual diplomacy, the one official and the other secret. The official diplomatic service was duplicated by a secret organization, employing confidential agents and adventurers. It has been argued that this system, as perfected under the Regency by the Abbé Dubois, had certain advantages in that it broke with the old rigid traditions and introduced new currents into the somewhat stagnant waters of official diplomacy. Yet in practice it led to a variety of scandals and confusions,— of which that centering round the ambiguity of the Chevalier d'Éon was the most notorious,—and it rendered impossible that diplomatic certainty, which I have already defined as one of the essentials of good negotiation. We find Louis XV writing to the Marquis de Breteuil, the official French Ambassador in Russia;—'I realize your difficulty in reconciling the instructions you receive from me with those you receive from the Foreign Secretary.' Even those who are most hostile to the stuffiness inseparable from the professional diplomatist can scarcely contend that such a system of duplication is anything but destructive of sound negotiation. I should go so far as to contend that whenever a State seeks to run two foreign policies concurrently,—a temptation to which despots and Prime Ministers are specially liable—then diplomacy becomes immediately ineffective. Again and again, from the days of Demosthenes to the days of Lloyd George, and Neville Chamberlain, has history taught this seemingly simple lesson.

But I have observed that politicians, unlike diplomatists, have no time to learn the lessons of history.

# IV

## THE TRANSITION BETWEEN THE OLD
## DIPLOMACY AND THE NEW

I

I HAVE dealt hitherto with three samples of diplomatic
method, namely the Greek method, the Italian method
and the French method. In this my last lecture, I shall
consider what might perhaps be called 'the American
method', but what I prefer,—since the Americans have
not as yet discovered their own formula, to call,—'The
Transition between the Old Diplomacy and the New.'

By the French method I mean the theory and practice of international negotiation originated by Richelieu, analysed by Callières, and adopted by all European
countries during the three centuries that preceded the
change of 1919. I regard this method as that best
adapted to the conduct of relations between civilised
States. It was courteous and dignified; it was continuous and gradual; it attached importance to knowledge and experience; it took account of the realities of
existing power; and it defined good faith, lucidity and
precision as the qualities essential to any sound
negotiation. The mistakes, the follies and the crimes
that during those three hundred years accumulated to
the discredit of the old diplomacy can, when examined

at their sources, be traced to evil foreign policy rather than to faulty methods of negotiation. It is regrettable that the bad things they did should have dishonoured the excellent manner in which they did them.

In drawing attention to the virtues of the French method I am not of course proposing to scrap all existing machinery and to return to the system of the eighteenth or nineteenth centuries. The conditions on which the old diplomacy was based no longer exist. Yet there seems no reason why we, in recognising the faults of the old system, should ignore the many merits that it possessed. I am not, I repeat, suggesting that the old diplomacy should be reintroduced or even imitated: I am suggesting only that we should consider it objectively and with some realization that, as a method of negotiation, it was infinitely more efficient than that which we employ today.

Let me therefore consider five of the chief characteristics of the old diplomacy.

In the first place Europe was regarded as the most important of all the continents. Asia and Africa were viewed as areas for imperial, commercial or missionary expansion; Japan, when she arose, appeared an exceptional phenomenon; America, until 1897, remained isolated behind her oceans and her Doctrine. No war, it was felt, could become a major war unless one of the five Great European Powers became involved. It was thus in the chancelleries of Europe alone that the final issue of general peace or war would be decided.

In the second place it was assumed that the Great Powers were greater than the Small Powers, since they possessed a more extended range of interests, wider responsibilities, and, above all, more money and more guns. The Small Powers were graded in importance according to their military resources, their strategic position, their value as markets or sources of raw material, and their relation to the Balance of Power. There was nothing stable about such categories. Places such as Tobago or Santa Lucia, at one date strategically valuable, lost all significance with the invention of steam. At one moment Egypt, at another Afghanistan, at another Albania, would acquire prominence as points of Anglo-French, Anglo-Russian, or Slav-Teuton rivalry: at one moment the Baltic, at another the Balkans, would become the focus of diplomatic concern. Throughout this period the Small Powers were assessed according to their effect upon the relations between the Great Powers: there was seldom any idea that their interests, their opinions, still less their votes, could affect a policy agreed upon by the Concert of Europe.

This axiom implied a third principle, namely that the Great Powers possessed a common responsibility for the conduct of the Small Powers and the preservation of peace between them. The principle of intervention, as in Crete or China, was a generally accepted principle. The classic example of joint intervention by the Concert of Europe in a dispute between the Small Powers was the Ambassadors Conference held in London in 1913 at the time of the Balkan Wars. That Conference, which provides the last, as well as the best, example of the old diplomacy in action, prevented a Small-Power crisis from developing into a Great-Power crisis. I shall consider it under my next heading.

The fourth characteristic bequeathed by the French system was the establishment in every European country of a professional diplomatic service on a more or less identical model. These officials representing their Governments in foreign capitals possessed similar standards of education, similar experience, and a similar aim. They desired the same sort of world. As de Callières had already noticed in 1716, they tended to develop a corporate identity independent of their national identity. They had often known each other for years, having served in some post together in their early youth; and they all believed, whatever their governments might believe, that the purpose of diplomacy was the preservation of peace. This professional freemasonry proved of great value in negotiation.

The Ambassadors, for instance, of France, Russia, Germany, Austria and Italy, who, under Sir Edward Grey's chairmanship, managed to settle the Balkan crisis of 1913, each represented national rivalries that were dangerous and acute. Yet they possessed complete confidence in each other's probity and discretion, had a common standard of professional conduct, and desired above all else to prevent a general conflagration.

It was not the fault of the old diplomacy, by which I mean the professional diplomatists of the pre-war period, that the supremacy of Europe was shattered by the First World War. The misfortune was that the advice of these wise men was disregarded at Vienna and Berlin, that their services were not employed, and that other non-diplomatic influences and interests assumed control of affairs.

The fifth main characteristic of the old diplomacy was the rule that sound negotiation must be continuous and confidential. It was a principle essentially different from that governing the itinerant public con-

ferences with which we have become familiar since
1919. The Ambassador in a foreign capital who was
instructed to negotiate a treaty with the Government
to which he was accredited was already in possession of
certain assets. He was acquainted with the people with
whom he had to negotiate; he could in advance assess
their strength or weakness, their reliability or the
reverse. He was fully informed of local interests, prejudices or ambitions, of the local reefs and sandbanks,
among which he would have to navigate. His repeated
interviews with the Foreign Minister attracted no
special public attention, since they were taken for
granted as visits of routine. In that his conversations
were private, they could remain both rational and
courteous; in that they were confidential, there was no
danger of public expectation being aroused while they
were still in progress. Every negotiation consists of
stages and a result; if the stages become matters of
public controversy before the result has been achieved,
the negotiation will almost certainly founder. A
negotiation is the subject of concession and counter-
concession: if the concession offered is divulged before
the public are aware of the corresponding concession
to be received, extreme agitation may follow and the
negotiation may have to be abandoned. The necessity
of negotiation remaining confidential has never been
more forcibly expressed than by M. Jules Cambon,
perhaps the best professional diplomatist of this
century. 'The day secrecy is abolished,' writes M.
Cambon, 'negotiation of any kind will become
impossible.'

An ambassador negotiating a treaty according to the
methods of the old diplomacy was not pressed for

time. Both his own Government and the Government with whom he was negotiating had ample opportunity for reflection. A negotiation that had reached a dead-lock could be dropped for a few months without hopes being dashed or speculation aroused. The agreements that in the end resulted were no hasty improvisations or empty formulas, but documents considered and drafted with exact care. We might cite as an example the Anglo-Russian Convention of 1907, the negotiation of which between the Russian Foreign Minister and our Ambassador in St. Petersburg occupied a period of one year and three months. At no stage during those protracted transactions was an indiscretion committed or a confidence betrayed.

Such, therefore, were some of the distinctive characteristics of the old diplomacy—the conception of Europe as the centre of international gravity; the idea that the Great Powers, constituting the Concert of Europe, were more important and more responsible than the Small Powers; the existence in every country of a trained diplomatic service possessing common standards of professional conduct; and the assumption that negotiation must always be a process rather than an episode, and that at every stage it must remain confidential.

I trust that my preference for professional to amateur methods of negotiation will not be ascribed solely to the chance that I was myself born and nurtured in the old diplomacy. I am fully conscious of the many faults that the system encouraged. The axiom that all negotiation must be confidential did certainly create the habit of secretiveness, and did induce men of the highest respectability to enter into commitments which they did not divulge. We must not forget that as late as 1914 the French Assembly was unaware of the secret clauses of the Franco-Russian Alliance or that Sir Edward Grey, (a man of scrupulous integrity) did not regard it as wrong to conceal from the Cabinet the exact nature of the military arrangements reached between the French and British General Staffs. Confidential negotiations that lead to secret pledges are worse even than the televised diplomacy that we enjoy today.

Nor am I unaware of the functional defects which the professional diplomatist tends to develop. He has seen human folly or egoism operating in so many different circumstances that he may identify serious passions with transitory feelings and thus underestimate the profound emotion by which whole nations can be swayed. He is so inured to the contrast between those who know the facts and those who do not know the facts, that he forgets that the latter constitute the vast majority and that it is with them that the last decision rests. He may have deduced from experience that time alone is the conciliator, that unimportant things do not matter and that important things settle themselves, that mistakes are the only things that are really effective, and he may thus incline to the fallacy that on the whole it is wiser, in all circumstances, to do nothing at all. He may be a stupid man or complacent; there are few human types more depressing than that of Monsieur de Norpois or the self-satisfied diplomatist. He may be of weak character, inclined to report what is agreeable rather than what is true. He may be vain, a defect resulting in disaster to all concerned. And he often becomes denationalised, internationalised, and therefore dehydrated, an elegant empty husk. A profession should not, however, be judged by its failures.

### 2

I have seen it stated that the transition between the old diplomacy and the new began one hundred years before the revolution of 1919. According to this theory, the change is to be ascribed, not to President Wilson's egalitarianism or to Mr Lloyd George's faith in diplomacy by conference, but to the influence of three factors which had for long been operative but which exercised their maximum effect after the close of the Napoleonic wars. The first factor was the desire for colonial expansion; the second, intense commercial competition; and the third, the increased speed of communications. Each of these three did assuredly exercise an influence on the evolution of diplomatic method, but that influence was neither as quick nor as deep as has been contended. These three factors need to be considered.

As the successors of Louis XIV discovered too late, the desire for colonial expansion had a profound effect on foreign policy: its effect on diplomatic method was not so great. The principle of the Balance of Power, which was the dominant principle in the eighteenth and nineteenth centuries, caused statesmen to realize that it was imprudent, even when opportunity offered, to acquire too much. Thus in 1814, at a time when we were in the position to annex the colonial empires of France and the Low Countries, we find Castlereagh writing to Lord Liverpool as follows: 'I still feel doubts about the acquisition in sovereignty of so many Dutch colonies. I am sure our reputation on the Continent as a feature of strength, power and confidence, is of more real moment to us than an acquisition thus made.' It might be argued, I admit, that Castlereagh was not an imperialist and that the glories of a far-flung Empire assumed their most dazzling radiance only two generations later. The admirable principle that Castlereagh enunciated was certainly not adhered to in the scramble for Africa that thereafter ensued. The old tradition of the Balance of Power, and the diplomatic method that it has fostered, were thereafter complicated and compromised by new and uncontrolled appetites, by much flagrant hypocrisy, by fresh jealousies and suspicions, and by the perversion, as at the time of the Partitions of Poland, of the doctrine of a just equilibrium into a conspiracy for the sharing out of loot. This phase of imperialist adventurism was, in so far as we were concerned, brought to an end by the healthy shock of the South African War. It is true that the scramble for Africa affected policy more than it affected the method of negotiation. But during that excitable period the grandfather clock of the old diplomacy did certainly receive a jar; it never ticked with equal imperturbability again.

How far did commercial enterprise and the struggle to obtain markets and raw materials in their turn affect the old standards of professional diplomacy? As I have already mentioned when discussing the Venetian system and the French endeavour to secure a monopoly of the Levant trade, commercial ambitions and interests exercised an ever increasing influence upon foreign policy. It is only comparatively recently that they have produced an alteration in diplomatic method. Even in my own day, it was regarded by the older diplomatists as most improper that the German Government should use its Embassy at Constantinople to obtain concessions for German industrialists. It was not merely that those of the ancient tradition regarded it as undignified that diplomatists should concern themselves with questions of commerce: it was also feared that if commercial competition were to be added to political rivalry, the task of diplomacy would become even more complicated than it was already. The idea was that the several merchants should compete with each other, so to speak, unofficially, and should not look to their Embassies for any special assistance. This attitude may have been influenced by the fact that the old diplomatists realised that they were themselves not trained to deal with such technicalities. Since those days, a network of institutions and commercial attachés has been created, with admirable results for all concerned.

The speeding up of communications has certainly done much to alter the old methods of negotiation. In former days it took many months before a despatch could be received and answered and ambassadors abroad were expected to use their own initiative and judgement in carrying out the policy outlined in the instructions they had received on leaving home. Some ambassadors profited by this latitude to pursue a personal policy. 'I never,' wrote Lord Malmesbury, 'received an instruction that was worth reading.' Lord Stratford de Redcliffe, the 'Great Elche' at Constantinople, was personally responsible for Navarino, although not, as has sometimes been contended, for the Crimean War. Other highly gifted ambassadors, such as Sir Hugh Elliott and Sir Henry Bulwer, relished their independence as enabling them to indulge in personal eccentricities and romantic affairs. Yet these were exceptions. Most ambassadors during the period of slow communications were so terrified of exceeding their instructions or of assuming an initiative that might embarrass their home government, that they adopted a purely passive attitude, missed opportunity after opportunity, and spent their time writing brilliant reports on situations that had entirely altered by the time their despatches arrived.

Today a Foreign Secretary from his desk in Downing Street can telephone to six ambassadors in the course of one morning or can even descend upon them quite suddenly from the sky. Does this mean that a diplomatist today is no more than a clerk at the end of a line? Such an assumption would be much exaggerated. An Ambassador in a foreign capital must always be the main source of information, above all the interpreter, regarding political conditions, trends and opinions in the country in which he resides. In every democracy, in every cabinet or trade union, power at any given moment rests with three or four individuals only. Nobody but a resident ambassador can get to know these individuals intimately or be able to assess the increase or decrease of their influence. It must always be on his reports that the Government base their decision upon what policy is at the moment practicable and what is not. That in itself is a most important function and responsibility. But the ambassador also remains the chief channel of communication between his own government and that to which he is accredited. He alone can decide at what moment and in what terms his instructions can best be executed. It is he who, as

Demosthenes remarked, is in control of occasions and therefore, to a large extent, of events. Moreover he remains the intermediary who alone can explain the purposes and motives of one government to another. If he be foolish, ignorant, vain or intemperate great misunderstandings may arise and damaging indiscretions be perpetrated. Important results may depend upon the relations that during his residence he has been able to cultivate and maintain, upon the degree of confidence with which he is regarded, upon his skill and tact even in the most incidental negotiation. Nor is this all. An ambassador should possess sufficient authority with his home government to be able to dissuade them from a course of action which, given the local circumstances, he knows will prove disastrous. Governments who, in spite of the telephone and the aeroplane, allow themselves to be represented in foreign capitals by ambassadors to whose judgement and advice they pay no attention are wasting their own time and public money. No newspaper, no banking firm, would consider for one instant being represented abroad by a man in whose opinion they placed no confidence. I do not agree, therefore, that improvements in means of communication have essentially diminished the responsibility of an ambassador, or to any important extent altered the nature of his functions. Let me once again quote the words of M. Jules Cambon:

'Expressions,' he writes, 'such as "old diplomacy" and "new diplomacy" bear no relation to reality. It is the outward form,—if you like, the "adornments"—of diplomacy that are undergoing a change. The substance must remain the same, since human nature is unalterable; since there exists no other method of regulating international differences; and since the best instrument at the disposal of a Government wishing to persuade another Government will always remain the spoken words of a decent man (*la parole d'un honnête homme*).'

### 3

No, it was not the telephone that, from 1919 onwards, brought about the transition from the old diplomacy to the new. It was the belief that it was possible to apply to the conduct of *external* affairs, the ideas and practices which, in the conduct of *internal* affairs, had for generations been regarded as the essentials of liberal democracy.

It was inevitable, after the first World War, that some such experiment should be made. On the one hand, the ordinary citizen, being convinced that the masses in every country shared his own detestation of war, attributed the breach of the peace to the vice or folly of a small minority, which must in future be placed under democratic control. On the other hand, when the Americans arrived as the dominant partners in the coalition, they brought with them their dislike of European institutions, their distrust of diplomacy, and their missionary faith in the equality of man.

President Wilson was an idealist and, what was perhaps more dangerous, a consummate master of English prose. He shared with Robespierre the hallucination that there existed some mystic bond between himself and 'The People',—by which he meant not only the American people but the British, French, Italian, Rumanian, Jugo-Slav, Armenian, and even German peoples. If only he could penetrate the fog-barrier of governments, politicians and officials and convey the

sweetness and light of his revelation to the ordinary
peasant in the Banat, to the shepherds of Albania, or the
dock-hands of Fiume, then reason, concord and amity
would spread in ever widening circles across the earth.
He possessed, moreover, the gift of giving to common-
place ideas the resonance and authority of biblical
sentences, and, like all phraseologists, he became
mesmerised by the strength and neatness of the phrases
that he devised. During the long months of the Paris
Peace Conference, I observed him with interest, ad-
miration and anxiety, and became convinced that he
regarded himself, not as a world statesman, but as a
prophet designated to bring light to a dark world. It
may have been for this reason that he forgot all about
the American Constitution and Senator Lodge.

I have no desire at all to denigrate President Wilson,
who was in many ways inspiring and inspired. He
assumed a weight of responsibility greater than any
single human being is constituted to support, and he
was tragically crushed. Yet if we read again the tre-
mendous sermons that he delivered during 1918 we
shall find in them the seeds of the jungle of chaos that
today impedes and almost obliterates the processes of
rational negotiation. Let me, therefore, remind you, for
a moment, of some of the Fourteen Points, the Four
Principles, the Four Ends, and the Five Particulars.

The first of the Fourteen Points of January 8, 1918
provided that in future there should be nothing but
'open covenants of peace openly arrived at', and that
'diplomacy should proceed always frankly and in the
public view'. On reaching Paris, President Wilson
quickly decided that by 'diplomacy' he had not meant
'negotiation', but only the results of that negotiation,

namely treaties. He also decided that the phrases 'openly arrived at' and 'in the public view' were relative only and contained nothing that need deter him from conducting prolonged secret negotiations with Lloyd George and Clemenceau, while one American marine stood with fixed bayonet at the study door, and another patrolled the short strip of garden outside. I can well recall how startled I was, on first being admitted to the secret chamber, to discover how original was the President's interpretation of his own first rule. Today, being much older, I realize that the method he adopted was the only possible method which, in the circumstances, could have led to any result.

The general public, however, were not similarly constrained to test the validity of the President's pronouncements against the hard facts of international intercourse. They continued to assume that by 'diplomacy' was meant both policy and negotiation, and to conclude that, since secret treaties were demonstrably evil things, negotiation also must never be secret but conducted always 'in the public view'. This is perhaps the most confusing of all the fallacies that we owe to President Wilson.

In the second of the Four Principles of a month later, the President announced that the system of the Balance of Power was now for ever discredited and that subject populations must be granted their independence, irrespective of the wishes of other States. In the Four Ends of the following July he foreshadowed the creation of a League of Nations which would establish, to quote his words, 'the reign of law, based upon the consent of the governed and sustained by the organised opinion of mankind.' He failed to realize that the public is bored by foreign affairs until a crisis arises; and that then it is guided by feelings rather than by thoughts. Nor did he foresee that it would be impossible to organize the same opinion in every country simultaneously, or that the conscience of mankind, as a means of sustenance, might prove inadequate when faced by a dictator controlling all means of information. In the Five Particulars on September 27 he pronounced that the rule of justice which America must achieve would be one that 'plays no favourites and knows no standards but the equal rights of the several peoples concerned'. This commandment was subsequently misinterpreted to signify that not the rights merely, but also the opinions and the votes of even the tiniest country were of a validity equal to that of a Great Power. Egalitarianism was thus for the first time extended to imply equality among nations, an idea which does not correspond to reality and which creates mixed ideas.

If read as a whole, the successive pronouncements made by President Wilson during those months of 1918, constitute a magnificent gospel. They embody conceptions which no man should either ignore or disdain. The misfortune was that the public imagined that what was intended as a doctrine of perfectability was in fact a statement of American intentions. Thus when America repudiated her own prophet, a re-regrettable dichotomy was created between the realists and the idealists in every country. The former concluded that the whole of the Wilson doctrine was sentimental nonsense, and the latter floated off into vague imaginings that what they wanted to happen was likely to occur. As the latter were in the majority, the practical politician found himself in an invidious position. It was the endeavour to reconcile the hopes of the many with the doubts of the few that brought such seeming falsity to foreign policy in the twenty years between 1919 and 1939.

The Covenant of the League of Nations was none the less a very sensible document which, had it been applied with consistent strength, might well have established something like the rule of law among nations. The Secretariat created at Geneva by Lord Perth was a truly remarkable innovation, which, had general confidence been maintained, might have provided the world with a machine far preferable to that of the old diplomacy. The trouble was that this fine experiment was based upon a view of human nature which, had it been a correct view, would have rendered any League unnecessary. The ordinary peaceful citizen came to suppose that violence could be restrained by reason: it was not until it was too late that he understood that it could only be restrained by force. The old systems of authority, such as the Balance of Power, the Concert of Europe, and the discipline of the Great Powers, had been discredited; the new theory of reason proved incapable of controlling the unreasonable; in place of the old methods of stability, a new method of the utmost instability was introduced.

You may be thinking that in devoting so much space to the new ideas of 1919, I am transgressing my own principle and confusing policy with negotiation, theory with practice. You may argue that, even after President Wilson had sought to apply to international relations the principles of American democracy, the diplomatists continued undismayed to weave the old tapestry of alliances and combinations, of big or little *ententes*, of pacts and conventions. Yet you will agree, I think, that two important changes were in fact introduced into diplomatic method in the period that followed the war of 1914–1918. The first was the refusal of the American legislature to ratify a treaty negotiated and signed by their own chief executive in person. That assuredly was an innovation of the utmost significance and one that dealt a heavy blow to the sanctity of contract and the reliability of negotiation. The second was the increasing practice of indulging in the method of diplomacy by conference. By that I do not mean merely the several *ad hoc* conferences, such as Spa, Cannes, Genoa, Lausanne, Stresa and so on: some of these were necessary and some were not. I am referring rather to the permanent state of conference introduced by the League system and later by United Nations. These conferences do little to satisfy the vague desire for what is called 'open diplomacy'; but they do much to diminish the utility of professional diplomatists and, in that they entail much publicity, many rumours, and wide speculation,—in that they tempt politicians to achieve quick, spectacular and often fictitious results,— they tend to promote rather than allay suspicion, and to create those very states of uncertainty which it is the purpose of good diplomatic method to prevent.

The defects, or perhaps I should say the misfortunes, of the new diplomacy are today magnified for us as if on some gigantic screen. The theory that all States are equal, even as all men are equal, has led to lobbies being formed among the smaller countries, (as for instance between the Asians and the Latin-Americans) the sole unifying principle of which is to offer opposition even to the reasonable suggestions of the Great Powers. The theory that 'diplomacy should proceed always frankly and in the public view' has led to negotiation being broadcast and televised, and to all rational discussion being abandoned in favour of interminable propaganda speeches addressed, not to those with whom the delegate is supposed to be negotiating, but to his own public at home.

You will have observed that in these lectures I have made but slight reference to the diplomacy of the Soviet Union. Mr. W. P. Potjomkin, in his history of Diplomacy, assures us that the Russians possess one powerful weapon denied to their opponents—namely 'the scientific dialectic of the Marx-Lenin formula'. I have not observed as yet that this dialectic has improved international relationships, or that the Soviet diplomatists and commissars have evolved any system of negotiation that might be called a diplomatic system. Their activity in foreign countries or at international conferences is formidable, disturbing, compulsive. I do not for one moment underestimate either its potency or its danger. But it is not diplomacy: it is something else.

This may be a sad conclusion. But it is not my final conclusion.

It would, in my view, be an error to take as an example of modern diplomatic method the discussions that are conducted in the Security Council and the Assembly of United Nations. We may resent the wastage of time, energy and money: we may regret that, in transferring to external affairs the system of parliamentary argument, a more efficient type of parliament should not have been chosen as a model: we may deplore that the invectives there exchanged should add to the sum of human tension and bewilderment. Yet it would be incorrect to suppose that these meetings are intended to serve the purpose of negotiation: they are exercises in forensic propaganda and do not even purport to be experiments in diplomatic method. Such negotiation as may occur in New York is not conducted within the walls of the tall building by the East River: it is carried out elsewhere, in accordance with those principles of courtesy, confidence and discretion which must for ever remain the only principles conducive to the peaceful settlement of disputes.

It is not therefore either diplomacy by loud-speaker or diplomacy by insult, that we need consider, since these contain a contradiction in terms. It is whether the changes inspired, rather than introduced, by President Wilson in 1919 do not repeat and emphasize the defects of previous systems and render more difficult what must always remain the chief aim of diplomacy, namely international stability. Woodrow Wilson, with his academic intelligence and missionary spirit, did not realize that foreign affairs are *foreign* affairs, or that a civilisation is not a linotype machine but an organic growth. He believed that the misfortunes of mankind were due to the faults of statesmen and experts and that 'the people' were always right: he did not realize that, although it may be difficult to fool all the people all the time, it is easy to fool them for a sufficient period of time to compass their destruction. Thus if we examine the diplomatic method which I do not think it unfair to call the 'Wilsonian', or 'the American' method, we shall find that it omits many of the merits of the several systems that I have examined in these lectures and exaggerates many of their faults.

The chief fault of democratic diplomacy as practised by the Greek City States was its uncertainty. Not only were their diplomatic missions composed of delegates who betrayed each other, but the final decision rested with an Assembly whose members were ignorant, volatile, impulsive and swayed by emotions of fear, vanity and suspicion. No negotiator can succeed unless reasonable certainty exists that his signature will be honoured by his own sovereign. If either the conduct or results of negotiation are subject to irresponsible intervention or repudiation on the part of an Assembly, or even a Congressional Committee, then uncertainty is spread. My first criticism therefore of the American method is that it weakens certainty.

The fault of the method practised and perfected by the Italians of the Renaissance was that it lacked all continuity of purpose and represented a kaleidoscope of shifting combinations. It may be, for all I know, that the President, the State Department, the Pentagon and the Foreign Affairs Committee of the Senate, are unanimous regarding the aim to be achieved: but they are not unanimous as to the means to be adopted. The variability of the diplomatic method employed suggests opportunism rather than continuity: this is an unfortunate impression, a Machiavellian impression, for a great good giant to convey.

The French system possessed the great merit of creating a centralised authority for the formation of foreign policy and a professional service of experts through whom that policy could be carried out. The misfortune of the American system is that no foreigner, and few Americans, can be quite positive at any given moment who it is who possesses the first word and who the last: and although the Americans in recent years have been in process of creating an admirable service of professional diplomatists, these experts do not yet possess the necessary influence with their own government or public. The egalitarian illusions of the Americans, or if you prefer it their 'pioneer spirit', tempts them to distrust the expert and to credit the amateur. I am not just being old-fashioned when I affirm that the amateur in diplomacy is apt to be suspicious. 'Gullibility,' as Sir Edward Grey once said to me, 'is in diplomacy a defect infinitely preferable to distrust.'

Now that the old disciplines of Pope and Emperor, the old correctives of the Concert of Europe and the Balance of Power, have been dispensed with, it is regrettable that the authority exercised by the United States is not more consistent, convincing and reliable. Yet I am not pessimistic about the evolution of their diplomatic method. I know that the Americans possess more virtue than any giant Power has yet possessed. I know that, although they pretend to deride the lessons of history, they are astonishingly quick at digesting the experience of others. And, I believe that the principles of sound diplomacy, which are immutable, will in the end prevail, and thus calm the chaos with which the transition between the old diplomacy and the new has for the moment bewildered the world.